W9-CIF-166

How to Create
Sacred
Water

"*How to Create Sacred Water* is a must-have addition to your go-to library for personal growth and planetary healing. Ravenwood has adeptly crafted a powerful elixir of practical tools, inspirational stories, and heartfelt meditations and lovingly placed this guidebook on the altar, inviting each of us to add our magic, intention, and attention to the waters that flow through our bodies, emotions, and planet. I loved reading this book and will treasure it for years to come."

DANIELLE RAMA HOFFMAN, AUTHOR OF
THE TEMPLES OF LIGHT AND FOUNDER OF
DIVINE TRANSMISSIONS AND THOTH'S MAGIC ACADEMY

"Kathryn Ravenwood writes in a commonsense, down-to-earth style, yet she brims with elegance and depth. Weaving in her own remarkable and very human narrative, Kathryn gently but confidently encourages us to trust our own sacred essence and experience. She helps us find the potency of our own loving intention, our own consciousness, our every action. She reminds us that all is one vast energy field and that we can be a healing force within it."

BRIAN C. TAYLOR, AUTHOR OF
BECOMING CHRIST AND BECOMING HUMAN

NOV 0 8 2012

"Raven is both companion and guide in this thoughtful journey through water and spirit. What a beautiful book!"

ALICE OUTWATER, AUTHOR OF
WATER: A NATURAL HISTORY

"*How to Create Sacred Water* is a blessing to the planet, at a time that we need it the most, when every day our waters become more polluted, more species become extinct, and our way of life and our planet are threatened. Thank you, Raven, for helping save the planet."

GLORIA TAYLOR BROWN, COAUTHOR OF
INVOKING THE SCRIBES OF ANCIENT EGYPT AND
CEO OF TAYLOR BROWN INTERNATIONAL

How to Create
Sacred
Water

A Guide to
Rituals and Practices

Kathryn W. Ravenwood

Bear & Company
Rochester, Vermont • Toronto, Canada

Bear & Company
One Park Street
Rochester, Vermont 05767
www.BearandCompanyBooks.com

Text stock is SFI certified

Bear & Company is a division of Inner Traditions International

Copyright © 2012 by Kathryn Ravenwood

All rights reserved. No part of this book may be reproduced or utilized in
any form or by any means, electronic or mechanical, including photocopying,
recording, or by any information storage and retrieval system, without permission
in writing from the publisher.

Library of Congress Cataloging-in-Publication Data
Ravenwood, Kathryn W.
　How to create sacred water : a guide to rituals and practices / Kathryn W.
Ravenwood.
　　　p. cm.
　Includes bibliographical references (p.　　) and index.
　ISBN 978-1-59143-141-1 (pbk.) — ISBN 978-1-59143-803-8 (e-book)
　1. Spirituality—Miscellanea. 2. Altars—Miscellanea. 3. Water—Religious
aspects. 4. Occultism. I. Title.
　BF1999.R38 2012
　203'.7—dc23

2012011558

Printed and bound in the United States by Lake Book Manufacturing, Inc.
The text stock is SFI certified. The Sustainable Forestry Initiative® program
promotes sustainable forest management.

10　9　8　7　6　5　4　3　2　1

Text design and layout by Virginia Scott Bowman
This book was typeset in Garamond Premier Pro, Avenir, and Legacy Sans with
Avenir used as the display typeface

To send correspondence to the author of this book, mail a first-class letter to the
author c/o Inner Traditions • Bear & Company, One Park Street, Rochester, VT
05767, and we will forward the communication.

This book is dedicated to the water.
Thank you, Water, for your gift of life.
I see you clean and restored.

Contents

Foreword

WHEN I FIRST SAW Kathryn Ravenwood's altar room and water altar shortly after 9/11/2001, I was humbled. Here was a person who not only talked the talk—she walked the walk in a most respectful and impeccable way. I was deeply impressed. Her commitment to Spirit was apparent in every object so carefully placed in her altar room, as was the time, care, and attention required to keep such a space alive and sacred. We exchanged gifts of magic and spirit that day, and her gifts to me included instructions for my own water altar, which continues to grace my altar space.

9/11 was a devastating tragedy that affected all of us in different ways. For me it was a time of hypersensitivity, yet I found myself numb, as though I, too, were dying. As soon as I could, I went into sacred ceremony, looking for a way to help, and found myself spinning into a dangerous mental state. After the ceremony my husband and I traveled north to a wedding in the San Juan Islands, stopping to visit Raven (as Kathryn is known to me) in Seattle on the way. I didn't realize how desperately I needed to immerse myself in the sacred nurturance of water. Yet Raven recognized it, and I bless her for it. Building and creating my water altar was a requirement for my sanity at the time. You don't have to wait until yours is threatened to create this sacred healing experience and deepen your relationship with water. This book will provide information and tools that will help.

I first met Raven in 1999. I was introduced to her by our mutual friend, Charla Hermann, a magical priestess and teacher who cofounded the Hawkwind Earth Renewal Cooperative in Alabama and is now directing its satellite center in Wyoming where Charla and Raven grew up together as childhood friends. Later that year Raven came to a weekend workshop on the goddess Sekhmet in Port Townsend, Washington. She continued to study with me at every opportunity until her first journey to Egypt, where she received the transmission to teach Alchemical Healing in our lineage of Thoth. She has since returned with me to Egypt and supported me many times during my travels, eventually assisting me wherever I taught if she was within driving distance. She carries special magic, especially around ceremony, as her connection with nature is profound.

The water altar that Raven shared with me, oh so many years ago, focused my awareness of the plight of the waters of the world, and awakened my resolve. Every time I traveled, I would take little bottles with water from my altar and exchange with the waters of oceans, seas, lakes, and rivers around the world—The Nile and Red Sea in Egypt, the Mediterranean, waters in Switzerland, Greece, Peru, and throughout the United States—wherever I went, so went the waters. After some years, I felt comfortable to share my water altar with others in certain of my classes and retreats. I'm so glad this book now makes the instructions available so that others can have direct guidance from Raven regarding this and other valuable spiritual work.

Remarkably, last summer one of my associates who had started her water altar during one of my retreats, created an opening ceremony for the main stage of the Oregon Country Fair, an iconic festival that has been happening near Eugene, Oregon, since the late 1960s. The intricate ceremony she directed was designed to honor the waters of the world. It included water from her altar and mine and even spawned

A water altar at the Oregon Country Fair
(Photo by K. Indigo Ronlov)

seven new water altars to be honored in different locations around the fair. These water altars are held (that is, tended and nurtured) throughout the year by people aware of the power of the prayers we send out in this way.

The water altar work is only one of the gifts you will receive from this book. I believe that readers of this book are serious about serving Spirit and, through their service, helping to heal our planet. I know that you will find great value in this book, and that when you take the journeys and initiations, and if you choose to start and maintain a water altar, your focused intention and prayers will become one with the sacred waters of life and with the intentions and prayers of the many others who are doing this and similar work. Together we will make a difference.

It is an honor to write the foreword for *How to Create Sacred Water: A Guide to Rituals and Practices*. The privilege is made more distinctive because this book is so good; beautifully written, informative far beyond the expectations of its title, abundant with rich stories, and quite clear in its instructive approach to the many ways we can honor water as a truly sacred and precious substance. And, as if that weren't enough, Raven is able to translate her own magical experiences into shamanic journeys (guided visualizations) so that you can directly experience initiations and rites that will transform your relationship not only with water but with all of nature and Spirit.

NICKI SCULLY

Nicki Scully has been a healer and teacher of shamanism and the Egyptian mysteries since 1978. She lectures worldwide and specializes in spiritual tours to sacred sites in Egypt, Peru, and other countries. She is the author of *Alchemical Healing: A Guide to Spiritual, Physical, and Transformational Medicine* and coauthor of *Planetary Healing: Spirit Medicine for Global Transformation*.

Preface

WE LIVE IN A TIME of extremes. Weather disasters have become common. Drought plagues one area while a neighboring state or country is flooded. We hear about climate change, Earth changes, the ending of ancient calendars, and coming shifts in consciousness. More people speak of expanded consciousness and transformational living while millions still live with limited awareness of anything beyond their dire, immediate physical needs or egos besot with materialism.

This book is about an evelation. What is an evelation? It is a revelation that evolves someone into a higher state. I experienced an evelation regarding water that caused me to create my sacred water altar and led me into an entirely new relationship with water. It also reshaped my life. Water cannot flow without making a change in the area it passes through; neither can Spirit.

How to Create Sacred Water is the story of my evelation. It is also a manual of simple instructions anyone can follow to help with the transformation of the waters of the earth. Every person can make a difference and can help in restoring the balance. We are all connected; what happens on the inside is reflected in our exterior world. The outside world floods us with the energies and events happening across the globe. No one is immune. No one is excused.

Besides an instruction manual, *How to Create Sacred Water* offers a series of spirit journeys to help connect or reconnect to Spirit through guides who offer their loving assistance to us in our personal life journeys, and offer suggestions as to how we can be the change that is so needed. As many times as we reach out, Spirit is there to connect with us, teaching us something new about ourselves, our world.

There are many ways to learn and transform. Keeping a sacred water altar in your home opens a portal to new dimensions. I invite you to walk through that portal, to explore, bless, and be blessed.

Acknowledgments

MY THANKS TO EVERYONE at Inner Traditions • Bear & Co. for believing in this book.

I am blessed with fabulous friends. Spirit flows through them to me in boundless blessings, gales of laughter, strength for the journey, and profound wisdom. This book could not have happened without you. Charla Hermann, we discovered the road out of Wyoming was riddled with detours and that we had no map. Thanks for a forty-two-year road trip. Gloria Taylor Brown, I don't know how you saw all those good things in me but thanks for dragging them out, even when I balked, and for being the best of mentors. You are wizard of the practical, goddess of the visionary, and you wear them well! Nicki Scully, teacher and guide, prankster and priestess, you gave me Egypt, the best gift ever. Cosmic girlfriend thanks to Normandi Ellis, the muse of muses who opened the Book of Words within me. Who knew a Kentucky girl could be so much fun! A big thanks to Samee and Nancy for test-driving the journeys and to Misha and Annie for keeping me on track and accountable. Diana, our long walks, amazing talks, and trips to Whole Foods sustained me. You are all spirit sisters extraordinaire.

To my son, Jason, thanks just for being here. You make my world brighter.

Much love and gratitude to my family. I hold you all in deep respect for your lifestyle and dedication to the Mormon religion. Thanks for embracing me even though my path went in a different direction.

1

The Monster

ON A SULTRY SEPTEMBER DAY in 1999 off the coast of Africa, the waters of the Atlantic Ocean spawned a monster of mythic proportions. This monster did not rise up from murky, uncharted depths as a hideous sea creature rearing multiple heads, devouring terrified tourists on cruise ships. It was not a gigantic fish with jaws full of razor sharp teeth gnashing at unsuspecting swimmers. It had nothing to do with revengeful ghosts of pirates who came to the end of violent lives by walking the plank; their last footsteps falling into thin air, scrabbling against gravity as they plunged into their waiting watery graves.

No. This monster was born as a single tropical wave sparkling in the sunlight, drinking in the hot, solar rays beaming down into it. Its appetite for heat could not be sated. It continued to suck the sun's fiery outpouring into the open vessel of the ocean. Launched along with the movement of the water, the monster began to take form, reaching out with vaporous tendrils to snag currents of cooler air drifting unsuspectingly above.

A cosmic dance began. Gentle, graceful twirls between water and air accelerated into a frenzied whirl. The surface of the ocean quickly became insufficient as a dance floor. Demanding more room, the monster launched itself skyward and began to spin counterclockwise across

1

the Atlantic toward San Salvador. Dancing up a storm, it dropped in on the Bahamas leaving its calling card of disaster and destruction behind on Abaco Island. A right turn steered the monster toward the North Carolina coast of the United States. Giant arms wheeled out of massive clouds as it turned in indescribable power. Experts around the world, who knew and judged the fine points of such dancing techniques, clustered themselves around computer monitors, watching in rapt fascination. Sufficiently impressed, they awarded the performance with high points, rating it a storm category between four and five, and gave the monster a name: Hurricane Floyd.

Floyd traveled with an entourage. Vast amounts of rain preceded its arrival in North Carolina, dropping between 15 and 20 inches onto land already oversaturated from Hurricane Dennis's deposits just ten days earlier. There was no welcome for Floyd, no place for its unwanted deluge and 130 mile per hour winds.

Floyd came anyway, making landfall at Cape Fear, North Carolina, on Thursday, September 16, 1999, at 6:30 a.m. as a category 2 hurricane. Storm surges 10 feet high slammed the coast tossing boats around, smashing them into piers that splintered and collapsed into the roiling waters. Trees, uprooted by all the rain, toppled over, smashing homes and cars, yanking utility lines out of the sodden ground. People, nerves and resources worn-out from a season of storms, fled to higher ground. Floyd howled and hurled, wreaking havoc in unrelenting fury.

By nightfall, it seemed the worst was over. Exhausted and wary, those people who rode out the storm crawled into their beds for a few hours of fitful sleep. But like a bad dream, Floyd was not done yet.

With silent stealth, Floyd snuck back in through the dense system of rivers, creeks, and streams that circulated North Carolina's usually peaceful and beautiful waters. That night the Tar, Neuse, Roanoke, and Pamlico Rivers and all their tributaries, swollen with Floyd's inundations, could no longer hold back the surging water. With the worst of timing for the weary residents, the rivers all overran their banks. Around 2:30 Friday morning the local fire departments drove their trucks through the rural neighborhoods, honking horns, blowing sirens, and bringing more bad news: the rivers were flooding. It was time to evacuate.

The flood now ran directly through the heart of North Carolina's pig and poultry production farms where millions of chickens, turkeys, and hogs were held captive in low-roofed containment houses, being raised in mass production for the meat industry. On each farm were lagoons to collect and hold the waste products of thousands of animals. The word *lagoons* was simply a corporately chosen euphemism for open sewage pits. Dug directly into the earth, many directly on the flood-plain of a major river, these pits were approximately 12 feet deep and 4 or 5 acres wide. Lined only with plastic, the engineering of the sewage lagoons depended on gravity to pull the heavy, raw sludge to the bottom, acting as a sealant against leakage. Each one held about 25 million gallons of raw fecal matter and urine. The lagoons were infested with undigested heavy metals, growth supplements, hormones, pesticides, parasites, and antibodies that had passed through the caged animals' bodies.

Floyd's floodwaters gushed into and through the buildings-turned-death traps, drowning the terrified animals en masse, and smashing away all structure. The collection lagoons were completely washed out, flushing the poisonous potion directly into the waterways.

Not satisfied with the carnage, the ravaging waters swept through sewage plants, spilling human filth into the torrent. Dozens of dams along the engorged rivers were damaged or destroyed, spilling more volume into the putrid flood. Even 225 caskets were pulled from the ground and sent downstream. Gasoline, motor oil, pesticides, fertilizers, cars, tractors, homes, precious topsoil, and failed dreams all spewed together into a toxic soup. Entire towns were covered with it.

The rivers crested as high as 24 feet above normal flood stages, surpassing records set in 1919. Days later, when the waters finally began to recede, 18,000 square miles of North Carolina were under water. The afflicted area had become a giant estuary filled with levels of fecal coliform bacteria so high that residents could not drink, cook, or bathe in the water. The liquid filth had nowhere to go except into the flooded rivers, wetlands, and then into the ocean. The water supply of every living creature in its path was contaminated. Hundreds of farms were destroyed.

Massive evacuations prevented all but fifty-seven human deaths, but the body count was astronomical. The death toll included 2.2 million chickens, 737,000 turkeys, 30,500 hogs, and 250 horses. Bulldozers were brought in to scrape up towering piles of bloated bodies reeking in the steamy and stinking air. Attempts were made to incinerate the mountains of corpses. Fires roasted the dead flesh twenty-four hours a day in three counties but could not get ahead of the rotting process. The digging of mass graves began when incineration failed; but the water table had risen to the surface of the soggy ground. The digging just caused more of the polluted water to ooze, squishing around the equipment, making sickening sucking sounds. With entombment impossible, the bodies were left to rot in sludge-covered fields or were swept out through the waterways toward the ocean, littering the landscape with death, decay, and disease.

There was nothing more that could be done.

The monster born on an African wave had carved its indelible mark across the southeastern United States. Things would never be the same.

2

The Voice

THE BALD EAGLE perched patiently on a dead branch at the top of the tallest tree on Duck Island. From this lofty perch, it could survey all the action across the serene September waters of Greenlake, a popular and particularly lovely park in Seattle, Washington. The eagle's white head feathers flashed in the sun streaming through a vivid blue sky. Its head rotated to observe a crowd of crows making a ruckus a few trees over. Keen hearing picked up the muffled laughter of brightly clad joggers making their daily run around the circular 3 1/2-mile lake pathway. A slight breeze gently ruffled the majestic bird's glossy brown feathers and sent little waves across the surface of the lake.

A green-headed mallard duck fluttered brightly patterned wings, reached its orange webbed feet out toward the cool water, quacking its arrival as it made a routine splash landing. In an instant, the acutely alert eagle spread its 6-foot wing span, launched itself off the branch, and dived straight down after the duck. It was a no contest event. The raptor dined richly on its reward.

Seattle has a reputation for gray skies and rain. It is less known for, and residents try to keep secret, the fact that September can be the best of weather anywhere. On one of those rare and gorgeous days, I began a never imagined journey with a casual walk around Greenlake.

Middle age was being good to me. Ten years before saw me graduating from massage therapy school, starting up a practice, and finding out I was very good at my chosen craft. I enjoyed a life focused on health, healing, and consciousness expansion. Supported by a community of interesting, creative, and intentional people, I was exploring my spirituality. Part of that exploration was participation in a monthly gathering focused on planetary healing where we offered prayers for the Earth. We referred to Mother Earth as a conscious being, Gaia, as she was called in the ancient Greek pantheon. The usage of that name had been revived in recent years in the alternative spiritual communities.

To me, Gaia was more than a Greek myth. I pictured her as the most beautiful of dancers, clad in a flowing emerald-green gown, gliding gracefully in her path around the sun. Her body was shaped of majestic mountains, her shoulders draped with shawls of pure white snow. Lush valleys of grasses and flowers were her hair, expanses of deserts and grasslands her swirling skirts. The night skies were her eyes, the sounds of the winds her voice. Arteries of oceans, rivers, and waterways carried her life force to all her children. The two-legged and four-legged, the winged ones, those who swam or crawled, the trees, the rocks, and the elements were all living beings interconnected in the great and beautiful life Gaia supported.

Today at Greenlake on this perfect, late summer day, the sunlight created sparkling diamonds on the gently dancing waves. Bright red paddle boats, silent except for an occasional splash, dotted the lake. Strong-armed rowers from Greenlake Crew, in sync with the rhythmic call of the coxswain, dipped their oars in and out of the water as they propelled long, brightly colored boats across invisible water lanes dividing their passage into safe distances from canoes and other nonmotorized craft that shared the lake. Bicyclers, parents pushing baby strollers, roller skaters, and walkers shared the two paved lanes around the lake. Patient fishermen coaxed brown trout onto their lines. The wading pool was filled with kids of all ages engaging in good-natured splashing, enjoying the refreshing water on a warm day. Even the Seattle Police Department's bicycle cops, patrolling the lake circle on their black bikes, clad in black uniforms and helmets, seemed festive.

Stepping off the path onto the soft green grass shaded by tall trees, I stopped to cradle the lush, low-hanging branches of a cedar in my hands. The tree's rich resins emitted its unique and pungent scent. Rubbing a little of the sticky substance on my hand so the smell would stay with me, I sat down and drank in the beauty of my surroundings. Redwing blackbirds sang their distinctive song. A great blue heron hid in the higher grasses at the edge of the water watching for fish to swim by and become lunch.

Watching the heron reminded me of the news reports I had recently heard of Hurricane Floyd hitting North Carolina, devastating the animals and the water. The images in my head created a sharp contrast to the idyllic scene around me. What did two million dead chickens look like? I pictured the animal carcasses, fertilizer, and gasoline swirling around in the floodwater and wondered how much pollution was too much. How many dead animals could the natural filtering process accommodate? Was it possible to clean up from such a grizzly toll?

What was happening to Gaia?

I felt helpless. What could I do way up here in the Pacific Northwest?

Just then I heard a voice in my right ear, as clearly as if someone sitting next to me had spoken. "You know, you could make a crystal homeopathic elixir that would heal the waters of Gaia." To say my reaction was one of surprise would be an understatement. What the heck? Am I hearing things? My body went on full alert. My senses perked up as if tasting the air, evaluating my situation. There was no one talking to me; did I imagine the voice? A great sense of clarity came over me. It was not my imagination. I did hear that voice.

Although I trusted my intuition and used it successfully in my massage work, my experience with audible instructions from an unseen origin was limited. My spiritual training supported the concept of receiving communication from a higher source—call it Spirit—that would bring guidance and assistance if we could just tune in to it. Still learning about this kind of communication, it was somehow more believable that visions and messages happened for other people, not me. I had great confidence in my ability to treat a client for whiplash or a rotator cuff injury but I was not so confident in my still-burgeoning spiritual gifts. Listening to voices was an undeveloped talent for me.

And yet, the voice had spoken and I had heard it. I could not deny it. This very clear direction was happening to me. Right now. During our lives we come to crossroads, turning points, where the next steps lead us onto new pathways and directions. The voice put me right at the junction of such an opportunity. I stepped forward. I believed.

I don't know how long I stayed in this somewhat altered state but, eventually, I got up and continued the circular walk around the lake, returned to my car, and drove home. The message haunted me. How would I make a crystal homeopathic elixir to heal the waters of Gaia?

And what was that, anyway?

3

Rocks and Pellets

I HAVE BEEN DRAWN TO ROCKS and crystals since I was a small child. I grew up in Wyoming with rocks everywhere. Even though we lived in Casper, one of the biggest towns, undeveloped areas stretched out through our neighborhood providing unlimited opportunities to ride my bike on dirt pathways or out onto the nearby prairies, where I spent blissful summer days hunting for lizards and collecting rocks. Even the alley behind our house was a treasure lane filled with sparkling stones. I liked to gather those that caught my fancy, take them into the back-yard, and run water from the garden hose over them. The water exposed their secret bands of colors as they went from dry and dusty to gleaming wet. I never got tired of playing with them.

I used to beg my mother to drive me to the local rock shop that was all the way across town by the airport so I could explore its vast inventory and hold the beauties in my small hands. She would not always indulge me, making adult excuses like "it takes too long" or "I'm busy" and other such things that really made no sense to me. What could be more important than looking at rocks?

When she would finally agree to go, it was a great adventure for me. It seemed to take forever to get there. Once we left the main part of town and got onto the highway, the great wide-open spaces of Wyoming were on display. Small herds of antelope roamed around the open prairies. Sagebrush waved in the constant wind. The local mountain range rose majestically and stretched along the southern edge of town. There were lots of rocks up on the mountain, too. Maybe I could get Mom to drive us there soon.

The anticipation of what I would find when we finally got to the little shop tantalized me. Not a fancy store in any way, it was more of a Quonset hut, its four basic walls topped with a corrugated metal roof. Single-pane windows let in the Wyoming sunshine and allowed the notorious wind to push occasional gusts of air past dried-up window caulking creating drafts and little puffs of dust. Tall shelves lined the walls and stretched across the large display room. Spiders, rarely noticed or bothered by anyone, spun layers of cobwebs draped from bare lightbulbs to piles of old boxes, connecting the corners of the ceiling with their silky threads.

The store smelled like dirt; like heaven. The treasures those four walls held were miracles to me—rose quartz, clear quartz, geodes cut in half exposing magical star-shaped centers, thinly sliced pieces of moss agate with feathery veins looking like ancient fern plants encased in see-through stone, yellow stones, black stones, and speckled stones. Fossils filled with bits of plants and animals from ancient seas held a great fascination and, oh, those crystals with their spikes sticking up out of their round or oval bodies! I loved them all. I would hold them, smell them, even put my tongue on them to taste them if Mom or the shopkeeper wasn't watching me.

Finally, agonizing over the many choices, I would select one or two beauties and trade them for my money, saved from shoveling snow during the winter or any other chores I could manage to do for pay. Counting out the coins, the shopkeeper would ring up my purchase, wrap my selected treasures in newspaper, and hand them over to me. They were like friends; like family. The ride home seemed to go by fast. When we got to the house I would run to my bedroom, carefully arrange my treasures on a shelf, and bask in their presence.

This love of rocks and crystals stayed with me as I grew up. From my spiritual studies, I learned to refer to them as the Stone People, part of Gaia's family. They lived in my home with me, sitting on windowsills where the light could shine on them. I also used them at the massage clinic as part of my treatment regimens. These were special tools; smoothed, cylindrical wands specially carved from beautiful, high-quality stones specifically designed to be used in massage treatments. These wands fit comfortably in my hands and felt like extensions of my own body. They provided a new dimension to the work I was doing. In addition to their specific design, I discovered that the stones had their own individual qualities. Different stones worked better for different parts of the body. These tools were not just to smooth out knots in the muscles, they were causing changes to the energy I could feel around the body. My clients loved them. They enhanced the healing experience I could offer.

After each treatment I washed the wands, dried them, and placed them on a clean towel. The act of caring for them was reminiscent of my water play with rocks as a little girl. And, it made me think about the voice's suggestion of making a crystal homeopathic elixir to heal the waters of Gaia.

That voice. What was I supposed to do? It had been a couple of weeks since I heard it at Greenlake and I had not yet figured out what it was about. The feelings I had around this were strong. I knew it was important. I wanted to pursue it. But how? What did crystals and homeopathic medicines have in common?

I had not received further instructions from the voice regarding this elixir so I decided I had better do some work on my own. Maybe I needed to let Spirit know I was willing to learn and make the effort to take on something new. It was time for research.

I got out my books on homeopathic medicines to review how they are made. In my own personal healing, I had used these remedies for about ten years as an alternative, natural medicine; keeping bottles of the small white pellets on hand in the medicine chest for a variety of common ailments such as a cold, sore muscles, flu, or bug bites. As my first choice for self-treatment, I found them very effective. Originally introduced by German physician Samuel Hahnemann in 1796, homeopathics addressed the body's needs in subtle, energetic ways. Simplified, the premise is that the body is healed by what made it sick; a poison oak outbreak on the skin is healed with the homeopathic remedy made from poison oak. The process of creating the remedies begins with the introduction of a component, such as poison oak, into purified water. After the substance is placed in the water it is stirred repeatedly, creating heavily diluted preparations until the water becomes an energetic resonance of the original substance placed in the water. The water is then infused into a pill or pellet that holds the remedy. A basic tenet of homeopathic medicine is that each dilution increases the effect of the treatment. This process is called *potentization*.

It is as if the water has memory that retains the original component through all the dilutions.

While I didn't understand why or how, this process seemed like an important part of the voice's message to me. I felt stronger about its suggestion each day. I did not know the answers—just that crystals and water would be involved in the creation of this elixir. I found myself going deeper into a sacred trust: if Spirit wants me to do this then Spirit will show me how to do it.

4

The Discovery

ON A DAY BUSY WITH CLIENTS and needing a break, I walked to the nearby shops in Ballard, the local neighborhood, during my lunchtime. I strolled by an antique-and-consignment store called Annie's, where I frequently enjoyed browsing. Just outside the store the voice returned:

"You know, you could go into Annie's and see if there are any crystals there."

After waiting and waiting to hear this voice again, when it finally returned my response was not what I would have predicted. I actually began to argue with it! What happened to my saying yes to Spirit? I must have looked like a crazy woman because I think I was actually talking out loud.

"Why should I go in there? They don't have any crystals in there."

And Spirit (ultimately patient) said, "Well, you could go in and look."

Again I said, "But they don't have things like that at Annie's."

Spirit raised its voice and said, "Just go inside and look!"

In I went.

The store was full of retro clothing, old furniture, antique glass and china, sets of silver flatware, and all sorts of unique cast-off treasures waiting for new homes. A faint musty smell clung to old carpets and fur coats. Two dressing rooms draped with colorful fabric for doors provided privacy for trying on vintage outfits. Shopping at Annie's was a lot like playing dress up—creating oddly matched ensembles of old velvet hats, silk blouses, bejeweled jeans, and cowboy boots.

The woman behind the counter looked up as I came in. I could see a glimmer of concern cross her face; I was probably still muttering excuses to Spirit! As if being reeled in like a trout on a spinning rod, I walked directly to a glass display case across the room. Inside was an amazing piece of amethyst crystal practically shouting out my name. Next to it was what looked to me like a short crystal wand. Oh my.

I felt as if I had walked through some kind of invisible barrier into another dimension. I had never seen crystals at Annie's and yet, there they were! Just like the voice said. I immediately purchased the amethyst. It was large, heavy, slightly bigger than the size of a cantaloupe cut in half, flat-bottomed, and rounded on the top. White bands of quartz were laced through the beautiful purple points of crystal clustered tightly together. The price was low compared to similar-size crystals I had seen in the New Age stores. It seemed that Spirit had set this up to make it easy for me.

But the other stone confused me. I didn't know what it was. About 6 inches long, rectangular in shape, and maybe ¹/₂ inch thick, it was cloudy white in color and textured in layers that looked as if they could be chipped off without much effort. It wasn't quartz, I knew that, and somehow I thought it should be. Maybe it wasn't even a real crystal. It was probably some synthetic, a fake. After all, this was a consignment store. People brought in all kinds of stuff. The amethyst was a sure thing; best not to get distracted by an unknown rock—or whatever it was. I must have passed from the dimension of spirit guidance back into the analytical realm of my own mind because, after much deliberation and many strange looks from the store clerk, I did not buy the unidentified rock.

I left Annie's with the amethyst wrapped up in newspaper and went back to my massage clinic, excited that the voice had indeed led me to what must be the next step of the journey. It was like being on a cosmic scavenger hunt. I followed the clues and found a great prize. The feeling that something special was happening was tingling all through my body! Standing at the counter in my massage room, I unwrapped my crystal treasure and began to rinse it under cold water in the sink. Then, very clearly, the voice spoke again:

"Why didn't you buy the wand?"

Uh-oh. Doubt dashed down the excitement of the moment.

I answered, "Well, I don't know what kind of crystal it is. I don't think it is quartz."

Like that lame answer was going to appease the voice!

Sure enough, I heard, "Go back."

I hustled out the back door and made a beeline to Annie's. The clerk looked somewhat distressed to see me again; I cannot imagine the expression on my face. But a customer is a customer so she indulged me, handing over what I now knew was a wand for inspection. I held it, peered closely at it, and turned it around in my hands. My mind once again took control. It was definitely not quartz and, considering that Annie's had its share of junk being passed off as authentic relics, I again rejected buying it. And all of this was within less than one-half hour's time! Yes, Spirit. No, Spirit. Who was in charge here, my ego or my higher knowing? What happened to that sacred trust?

I left Annie's empty-handed, returned to my clinic, and again began to rinse the amethyst in cold water to cleanse it. The amethyst-infused water poured over my hands. It felt as if the crystals had melded with the water, transforming it into a liquid purple that was flowing over and through my body. I felt a dimensional change come over me. I had never experienced anything like this before. It was as if the water had actually changed into something else and that my body was absorbing it.

Once again the voice said, a little louder:

"Why didn't you buy the wand?"

I had no reason. I just stood there in amazement. This was real! I was not reading about this in a book or hearing someone else's story. This was happening to me. Right now. Then the voice seemed to actually yell at me:

"Just go and buy it!"

I practically ran back to Annie's, feeling frantic. I could not believe myself! I was clearly guided to the crystals and was not following through. Whatever was the matter with me? As I approached the store, a man was opening the door to go in. Panic set in. Oh no! What if he buys the crystal? I rushed in, pushing past him, and went straight to the counter demanding to buy the wand. The saleswoman and the man looked at each other and then at me like I was from outer space. But the sale was finally made and, with much relief, I took the little wand to join its purple partner.

I stood at the small sink, rinsing both crystals and wondering, what's next?

Deepening Your Practice

In this chapter I argued with Spirit. In my life I consciously chose time for prayer and spirituality. I was a licensed healthcare practitioner, a massage therapist, focusing on assisting the healing process in my clients. I had studied metaphysical teachings for thirty years. I had the desire to deepen my awareness and connection to Spirit. Yet, my personality is such that I tend to approach my learning from a more intellectual level rather than experiential. This interchange with Spirit, which led me to discover the crystals in the antique store, required me to get out of my head. It stretched me beyond the imposed limits of my linear and logical mind and launched me into a new realm—of now, of trust, of action. When I finally stopped arguing, analyzing, and just said yes, the doors opened to a whole new world.

The process of learning to trust Spirit is part of our life journey. There are times when we feel very in tune and present with our higher selves, with Spirit. Other times we barge through our life experiences with our egos in charge, shutting out the voice. Our own self-doubt can also drown out the voice.

What are your hang-ups? What blocks you from hearing and allowing the voice of wisdom to guide you? Are you too dreamy? Too timid? Too controlling? Are you plagued by fear? Doubt? Ego? Logic? Whatever it is, you are not alone! We all have our challenges in living more conscious lives. Sometimes these blockages are so ingrained within us we don't even realize they are keeping us from enjoying a richer life. However, we need not continue to let our limitations define us. Every day is a new day; every breath a new beginning. As we learn to consciously set intentions for a more purposeful life, our thoughts begin to align with those intentions, helping us to make choices that result in more positive actions. Change is often more gradual than radical. Breath-by-breath, thought-by-thought, word-by-word, action-by-action we change ourselves; we create a better world.

5

Preparing to Journey with Spirit

THROUGHOUT THIS BOOK you will be invited to share in a series of spirit journeys, which are offered to you as guided meditations, to lead you to a vision or teaching from Spirit. Each journey has its own message to help you deepen your relationship with water. You can follow along in a way that works best for you. You may choose to read the words and experience the journey at the same time, or read the journey and recall it later as a meditation. You could journey with a friend or a group, one person reading for the other (or others). You might choose to read the text out loud, record it, and later follow your own voice as you journey. Whatever way you choose, it is my hope that you will experience firsthand how your prayers for the water, for Gaia, do make a powerful difference. You can create positive change in the world.

While on the journey you may not have the exact experience the words suggest. For instance, the suggested guide for a journey might be presented to you as Eagle. Instead of Eagle, your own personal guide might come to lead you. Go with what you are experiencing. You may not *see* the journey but might just know it is happening. The journey may guide you to a forest but you experience a different environment. This is all just fine. The important thing is to set an intention to receive the teaching intended in the journey. Your intention is the most important part. You may want to read through the journey first to help align your intention. Please do whatever is most comfortable for you.

I assure you these journeys have been offered with my full respect and gratitude for my own guides who have given these teachings to me, specifically for this book, to share with you. They are presented to honor Spirit, Gaia, and the water.

This kind of spirit journey meditation is also called *shamanic journey* work. It is not the focus of this book to attempt to train people as shamans. The journeys will, however, give you the opportunity to explore other realms of consciousness where Spirit can instruct you.

It took a lot of practice for me to learn to journey and trust what I was receiving. If you are new to this, be gentle with yourself. You may journey effortlessly or you may find resistance. It is all a learning process. If you are experienced in spirit journeying then proceed with intention in the manner you are accustomed.

Spirit offers a gift in each of the journeys. Accepting these gifts helps us to be receptive to Spirit. In each journey we are also asked to give a gift to the guide involved. This helps us remember to give back and honor our guides and teachers, the water, and all of life. Receiving and giving is the circle that keeps us connected to Spirit, brings us blessings, and helps us grow in consciousness and awareness to our higher purpose.

PREPARE TO JOURNEY

Turn off your phone and any other source of possible distraction. Allow yourself thirty minutes to an hour for the journey. Sit or lie down in a comfortable position. Next to your water altar is preferable (see chapeter 13), but you can be any place that is quiet and where you will not be interrupted. You might want a pillow or a blanket, but the intention is to journey out for teachings and vision, not to take a nap.

If you do fall asleep, just try it again later. I have heard lots of snoring in shamanic journey classes!

Each journey will begin by focusing on your breath. This will help your body and mind to relax, letting go of attachments to your physical surroundings, and allowing your higher consciousness to expand into the experience. No journey will ever suggest you do anything to compromise yourself in any way or to experience anything other than loving instruction from Spirit. During the journey it is important to pause after each sentence or instruction so that you will have the time you need to experience what is happening.

RETURNING FROM THE JOURNEY

Coming back from the spirit journey is not unlike returning home from a vacation. We need time to integrate the experience. If you are journeying with a friend, share your visions and teachings with each other. I suggest you start a spirit journey journal. Writing in a journal helps to recall more details and records the experience for future review. If you are an artist, you might choose to preserve your experiences by sketching out your visions, or even molding them in clay. If you have a powerful emotional reaction, such as tears, go ahead and cry. Let it out. Then write down how you felt. Allow Spirit to assist you in your growth. Sometimes we cry, sometimes we feel elated. Add these experiences to your spirit journey journal writings.

Drink some water. Share a light meal with your friends. It is best not to drive a vehicle right away. Give yourself a little time to get regrounded. If you feel very disoriented try this simple Grounding Breath breathing exercise:

Sit comfortably with your spine lifted up. Place both feet flat on the floor. Inhale and exhale. Visualize the chakras on the bottoms of your feet opening like little doorways. Inhale and exhale your breath down through these open doorways. Send your breath down beneath the floor, underground into the earth. Anchor your breath around a stone or tree root. Inhale this earth energy back up through your feet, back into your lungs. Repeat several times until you feel grounded.

6

Journey

Becoming the Vessel

WE EACH HAVE THE GIFT of communication with Spirit. This gift is called by many names: intuition; a gut feeling; the still, small voice; or an inner knowing. No matter what we call it, it is our personal connection to Spirit that opens the channels that allow us to access knowledge, wisdom, and warnings from a place outside our normal consciousness. This is not news. It has been experienced and written about throughout the ages. It is our human birthright. Spirit always keeps communication flowing. It is our responsibility to stay open and receptive. Sometimes that channel to Spirit is blocked by any number of distractions we encounter or create in our lives. The voice becomes hushed beneath our iPod tunes, TV shows, the latest app on our smart phone, focus on our jobs, or our generally very busy lifestyles. Emotional dramas can consume our energy. Taking time out of your day to sit in silence will help the voice come through. Sit with your water altar. Talk to the water. Pray. Keep an open mind. Learn to listen. Be receptive. I was just out for a walk when the voice came to me unexpectedly that day at Greenlake. I had a practice of prayer and quiet time but not a familiarity with allowing that voice to speak to me. I am so grateful I heard and listened that day!

We each are a vessel into which Spirit pours gifts. We are the hollow bone, as the Native elders call it, for Spirit to move through. When Spirit speaks to us it might be as a voice, through visions, or with insights and new ideas. It might be a subtle nudge or a major inspiration, but it will trigger something within us; perhaps through our studies, the work we do, or by helping us express our talents or our desire to be of service. I suspect that Spirit gives the same promptings to many people, all of whom might respond in completely different ways. One person might write a book and teach workshops, another might express the message through painting, sculpture, or music. Someone else might develop a new healing modality.

When we say yes to Spirit, doors open, we experience serendipitous events, and we have the opportunity to grow beyond our self-imposed limitations. The gifts we receive from Spirit are for giving back through our personal expression. The energy of life moves in a circle, or a loop. Spirit freely sends out the life force energy for all beings. As water in a vessel becomes stagnant if not circulated or refreshed, so we, as a vessel of Spirit, become clogged if we do not pour out our blessings to share with others and the earth. The more Spirit flows through us, the more we can receive and give.

Each of us is like a transmitter; we all receive the same life force energy but we broadcast that energy through our own unique frequency, using it as we choose. Hopefully we choose to use that energy to help us to grow spiritually, as well as to enjoy life. After all, joy is a big part of spiritual growth. It is through this growth and expansion that we use and spread the gifts of Spirit wherever we go, in whatever we do.

My experience with the voice and its ensuing lessons pushed my buttons. It challenged me in ways I had never anticipated. I chose to say yes and entered into a new relationship with water, with Spirit, and with myself. We are the agents of Spirit on earth; however, free will abides. We will not be forced. It is always our choice. What we choose creates who we become.

◎ Intention

The intention of this journey is to release accumulations and restrictions that restrict the flow of Spirit through us. The journey may bring an experience of a great catharsis or a simple feeling of purification. Releasing those blockages or layers within us at this time allows the energy that had been required in holding on to them to be used for a better purpose. We create a space for Spirit to enter and to fill that space with whatever is most needed: perhaps inspiration, forgiveness, love, clarity, or peace.

Breathe in. Breathe out. Allow your mind to quiet. Breathe in. Breathe out. Relax. Breathe. Allow your body to expand into the space created with your breath. Breathe. Let your consciousness expand. Breathe. Slip away to another place.

You are outside on a pleasant day in your yard, or garden. You are digging a hole in the ground, getting ready to plant flowers or a tree. You shovel into the earth, turning the soil so it will be loose, removing any large rocks or debris. Notice what the dirt feels like as you dig.

Your shovel clunks against something hard, creating a different sound than when you struck rocks. Curious, you put your shovel aside, kneel down, and begin to dig using your hands. How does the ground feel in your hands? Is it cold? Warm? Dry? Moist? Is it rocky or smooth? Does it have a smell to it?

As you dig around, your hands find a roundish feeling object. You want to see what it is so you pull it out of the ground. Is it easy to extract, or difficult? How does this object feel to you?

As you pull it out of the dirt, you discover it is a jar without a lid and is encrusted with dirt. Curious, you begin to rub the outside of the jar to clear the dirt away. The jar is layered with it; thick with it. You keep rubbing.

You turn the jar upside down, shaking out any loose dirt but find there are layers of encrusted dirt attached to the inside as well. You run your fingers around the inside as best you can but everything seems solid, stuck. What does it feel like to have your fingers inside the jar?

You go get the garden hose, turn the water on to a low flow, and fill the jar with water. Well, that is strange; you know the jar is encrusted with dirt but the water looks very clear. You dump out the water. The dirt is barely wet. You fill it again. Holding your hand over the top, you shake the jar, working the water into the dirt. The water is still mostly clear. You continue the process, adding water, maybe even scraping the sides of the jar with a stick. Finally, the water begins to loosen the hardened layers away from the glass. Notice what the dirt looks like as the water begins to turn it to mud. What does it smell like?

You add more water. Mud sloshes out of the jar. Bits of grass, small stones, and other debris are also loosened from the sides and bottom of the glass. It is a real mess but you can't stop now. You are totally intrigued, wanting to clean this jar, to see what it looks like. What is coming out of the jar with the mud?

Finally, you see the jar is getting clean. Excited, you keep washing and rubbing until it is completely clean of all the accumulated dirt. What does it look like? Is it clear? Does it have a color to it? What is its shape? Is it small or large? Long or thin? Is it heavy or light? Is it familiar? Have you seen this jar before? What does it feel like to hold it in your hands? Turn it around. Notice all you can about the jar.

You fill the jar with water again. The water is clean now. Notice how the jar holds the water. How the water conforms to the shape of the jar. Can you smell the water? You look down into the water and see your reflection in it. You bring the jar up to your mouth and take a drink of this water. Feel it pass your lips, go down your throat. Feel the water move inside your body. As you drink the water you realize the water is doing to you what it did to the jar. It is loosening blockages; loosening accumulated layers of resistance. Feel the water in your body.

Take another drink. Let the water cleanse you. Let the layers and blockages be purified with the water. Keep drinking the water. Let the water wash you clean. How does it feel to let these layers be washed away? What is being removed from you? As the layers wash away from you, where do they go?

You feel now that the water has washed you clean. You feel purified. You look again at the jar. As your efforts allowed it to become a vessel to hold clean water, you have become a vessel as well. Cleared of the layers and blockages, you are now open, empty, so you can be filled with the clean, pure waters of Spirit. Open yourself to receive the flow of Spirit. Welcome it into you. You feel Spirit flowing into you now like sweet, clean water; filling you, gracing you. You are becoming a vessel for Spirit. Let Spirit fill you. What does Spirit pour into you? How are you filled with Spirit?

As a vessel filled with Spirit you are now able to offer a drink to those who may be thirsting for what you have to share. What is it you have that you can offer to others? What has Spirit given to you? How can you share this with others so they may also clear away the layers inside them that block them from receiving Spirit's flow? Know that as you give to others you are refilled with Spirit's flow back into you. Feel the flow of Spirit through you.

Receiving these gifts inspires you to offer your gratitude in return. Offer your thanks to the water and to Spirit. Know that when you share your gifts and talents with others you are enhancing and bless-ing the flow of life.

As a vessel for Spirit you carry the precious flow within you. Know that you can be replenished by simply asking Spirit to enter and fill you. Knowing this, bring your attention back to your breath. Breath-ing in. Breathing out. Bring your attention back to your body in this time and space. And . . . you are back.

7

A Mormon Girl from Wyoming

THE INTELLECTUAL CONCEPT of hearing the guiding voice of Spirit was not new to me. I was raised in the Mormon religion. Mormons believe in modern-day revelation from God. However, that revelation is restricted to their prophet, the head of the church. Members are encouraged to listen to that still, small voice inside them when they are seeking answers to their prayers, to help them discern right from wrong. I do not recall being taught in Sunday school or seminary classes that I might personally receive a new teaching, or revelation. Revelations came to the prophet who then revealed them to the church members.

The Mormon Church has no liturgy, no paid ministry, and considers icons, such as a crucifix or an altar, to be idolatry. Being Christians, portraits of Jesus (as a white male with flowing hair) hang in the Sunday school rooms and are encouraged in the home. Pictures of Bible stories from the Old and New Testaments are fine, as well as those showing Book of Mormon scenes. Angels? Okay as long as it is the Angel Moroni. I never saw a picture of the angelic host, or Mary by herself. The closest thing to an altar was the sacrament table.

The Mormon Sacrament is the equivalent of the Holy Eucharist from the Catholic or Episcopalian Mass. Instead of wafers, white bread is used. Instead of wine, water. The Blessing of the Sacrament is the only prescribed prayer, the only ritual of Sunday services. This ritual is performed by males in the church who have been ordained into the priesthood. Priests of the church, who are males sixteen years of age or older, bless the Sacrament. Deacons, young boys of just twelve to fifteen years, pass the bread and water around to the congregation. One was not to partake of the Sacrament if one had been unworthy during the week. I presumed that meant if you were not being a good Mormon, you were not supposed to be blessed.

My disenchantment with the church came when I was about fifteen years old. I had a church friend, Charla, who was thirteen. We shared the annoying habit of asking too many questions. My parents clearly told me to "do what the Church tells us to do." My father also emphatically told me, while flicking his thumb and forefinger against my temple, to "use your head for something besides a hat rack." I was confused with these conflicting instructions; do as I am told or think for myself? Charla and I would talk about this in hushed asides when we were together at Sunday school. She was enough younger than I that we were not in the same school. The only time we had to talk was at church or at the Saturday night dances held in the church gymnasium twice a month.

The Mormons, like any organized religion, were fraught with hypocrisy. The church taught that complete obedience to the laws was the only way to obtain salvation. The hard part for me was that a woman cannot ever hope to obtain salvation without a man. Only men hold the priesthood and without the priesthood there is no ultimate salvation. Therefore, be a good girl and get married to a good Mormon man who holds your spiritual fate in his mortal hands. Just trust. Just obey.

Charla and I had a problem with that.

The Mormons like to socialize and the Saturday night dances

were a fun opportunity for young people to learn acceptable social skills while being closely chaperoned by adults. It was at the dances that Charla and I discovered that those priests, those boys who were only sixteen or seventeen, were very human. Having the honor of the priesthood did not seem to make them immune from sneaking outside to drink cherry vodka and then trying to cop a feel on the girls, us included. They were just normal boys but we had been taught they were like little demigods because of this special power they had that we could never experience. Somehow it was okay for the boys to break the rules but the girls were bad because we in some way encouraged it. The fault was ours; even when we clearly did not want or solicit such attention. We were afraid we would be punished if any of the adults noticed.

Charla and I quit taking the Sacrament on Sundays during the church service. Our parents never asked why. I am sure we broke their hearts as they thought we must be incredible sinners. We just refused to play the game.

I tried to be a good Mormon girl. I did everything I was told to do, but somehow I threatened my teachers by asking too many questions and wearing my skirts a little too short. I was continually singled out as an example of what not to do. Even our bishop took me into his office after observing me dancing in what he thought was a too daring manner at a church dance.

He told me, "girls like you are a dime a dozen. You had better straighten up and repent."

I was horrified. All I had done was cheek-to-cheek dancing during a slow song. The only other part of me that even touched my partner were my hands against his hands as we innocently danced to the Beach Boys. This felt like an inquisition. I was filled with both guilt and anger. There was a part of me that wanted to rebel. I had done nothing wrong; I knew that. Those boys at the sacrament table got to come back week after week to perform the great honor of their priesthood and I knew they were not following the rules. Why pick on me? But, I wanted to fit into this life. It was all I knew. I stuffed those emotions deep down and did what I was told.

I even went to Brigham Young University. Having excellent grades, I could have attended any school I wanted. I only applied to BYU and, of course, was accepted. I hated it almost immediately. I again experienced the silent taboo of asking questions. Just study, do what you are told, and find a returned missionary to marry. I came to understand that the real reason to go to college was not to get a B.A. or a B.S., it was to get your "MRS." Get married, have kids, be a good wife.

I eventually went into deep depression. By the second year, I was so miserable I could not even attend classes anymore. No one seemed to notice or care. My feeble attempts to reach out availed me no help. I called home begging to transfer to the University of Utah, in Salt Lake City, the mecca of Mormonism.

My father told me, "all schools are communistic except BYU. As long as I am paying the bills you will do what I say."

I cracked. "Fine. Then quit paying the bills." I dropped out and went home. My parents did not ask me what was wrong or how they could help. I don't think they knew how to do that. I was a mystery to them. My two older sisters were both BYU graduates, why was it so hard for daughter number three? So they walked on eggshells and ignored the elephant in the living room.

I tried going back to church. I even dated a returned missionary. It was assumed we would get married. You could feel the relief in the air. Charla was still in town, just finishing high school. At least I had a friend who understood me!

Looking back on major events in our lives, it is often apparent that there is one final moment that tips you over the edge, pushing you into the next part of who you are becoming. For me, it was the boyfriend. We were out on a date and he told me that I scared him.

"I scare you? Why?" I implored.

"Because you read. You think too much."

Oh no, not again. I went silent. Looking at him, thinking of spending the rest of my life with him was too much. I was done. When he took me home, we sat outside in the car. I took off the topaz ring he had given me and handed it back—broke up with him.

"But I thought we would get married," he whined.

"I wouldn't marry you if you were the last man on earth," I avowed. I got out of the car, slammed the door, and walked away from it all.

Charla and I eventually left Wyoming and the Mormon Church together in 1969, driving an old pink Studebaker sedan. We started out in Provo, Utah, so I could go back to BYU for a semester to rectify my incomplete grades and raise my GPA enough to transfer to a different school. That was not meant to be. I never even registered. Instead, we met up with the local hippies, started hanging out with them, and found out there were a whole lot of things the Mormon Church had not told us! We indulged in a new, liberating lifestyle that eventually led us to California.

It was the beginning of my personal quest for truth.

I had tools for the quest. I carried with me a Wyoming legacy of a deep love for the earth. I had many treasured memories of growing up there; being out on the open land, looking for horned toads to bring home as pets, collecting my precious rocks, or laying on my back watching the never ending parade of clouds passing through the vast expanse of blue above me. I like to think of Wyoming as the place where the cloud people go for their cloud conventions. During the summer, I slept outside in the backyard, wrapped in my sleeping bag, staring long into the night at the field of stars above me. From my position at over 5,000 feet elevation, the Milky Way was easy to see on dark nights, a starry road stretching into forever. I wondered who traveled along its shining path.

Growing up in Wyoming was a wonderful experience. The winters could be bitter cold with winds blowing hard enough to knock me down the hill as I walked to school, sometimes in temperatures of 50 degrees below zero. However, there was a great sense of freedom and wonder that I remember from living under the great blue skies in a state with only 350,000 inhabitants. As a kid in the 1950s I could safely spend long summer days riding my bike out on the prairies near our neighborhood. I rode out alone, with no particular place in mind, just exploring the wide-open spaces. As long as I was home by dinner I could do as I pleased. I loved the cottonwood trees with their gnarly trunks. Sagebrush grew in all open areas, waving in the wind. I would pull off branches of the pale green foliage and rub the plant on my arms, legs, and face, letting the fragrant oil permeate my skin, then stuff my pockets with it to bring the smell home with me. Decades later when I learned the ritual of smudging I had to laugh that I had known that as a child.

The Native American people were an integral part of the Wyoming population and culture, although not everyone honored them as sovereign nations or even respected them. My family enjoyed attending the state fair to watch the dancers from the Arapahoe, Shoshone, Sioux, and other tribes who gathered from Wyoming and neighboring states, camping near the fairgrounds in their teepees painted with symbols of the sun, buffalo, rain, lightning, and clouds. They proudly wore their beautiful regalia of ribbon dresses and shirts, moccasins, leather pants, and vests, decorated with intricately beaded motifs of flowers, birds, and animals. Some of the older chiefs had eagle bonnets that trailed feathers all the way down their backs. Singers and drummers sat around huge drums made from cottonwood tree trunks, beating out the rhythm of the dance, chanting in their native language. The dancers circled around shaking rattles, extending their arms out like eagle wings, their feet kicking up little clouds of dirt. I was fascinated by these ancient tribal rituals.

As I grew older, I learned more about some of the basic tenets of Native American spirituality—their reverence for the land, the water, sky, moon, sun, and animals. I developed a deep respect for them and a great sadness at how their world had been destroyed by the development of the Wild West and especially the almost complete destruction of the great buffalo herds.

I knew the spirituality of the Native Americans involved sacred vision quests. I wasn't sure exactly what a vision quest was except that the person doing the quest was usually a male. He would spend several days and nights alone in the wilderness, seeking a vision from his spirit guides. The vision provided guidance for the quester's personal life as well as for the lives of the tribe, or The People. I didn't know anyone who did this in real life, only from books I read. I delved deeper into Native American history and spirituality studies. Not having a teacher, I had to depend on books. The one that most influenced me was *Black Elk Speaks*, written by John Neihardt in 1932. Black Elk, an Oglala Sioux, shared the stories and visions of his life with Neihardt, including those around the Battle of Little Big Horn in 1876 and the Wounded Knee Massacre in 1890. Black Elk's vision of restoring what he called the sacred hoop of life awakened an old knowing within me. I learned from this book that all life was related: the animals, the land, the water, the sky above, and all that was in it. This connection was honored by saying thank you to all my relations. I felt deeply in tune with this concept of living life with an attitude and practice of earth-based spirituality.

The vision quest reminded me of the Mormon story of Joseph Smith, a young man of only fifteen years. Not knowing what religion of the day was the right one, Joseph went out to a grove of trees near his home to pray, seeking answers from God. Joseph had a vision in which he was visited by the Angel Moroni who gave him golden plates that were the Book of Mormon and would become one of the basic tenets of the religion Joseph would later found. Although I had separated myself from the Mormon Church, the idea of receiving a vision seemed perfectly natural to me. But why were only males getting to have that experience?

8

Ceremony and Sword

IN 1997 CHARLA INVITED ME to come visit her at her home in Alabama. She and her husband, Tarwater, owned a healing retreat there called Hawkwind where they taught different traditions supporting an earth-based spirituality. Tarwater was making drums, Charla was teaching women's rituals, and they were both apprenticing with Native American elders from different tribes, learning the old ways. They were having a gathering over a long weekend. She said it was time to bring me in. I did not know what she meant by that, but I was ready to find out. Flying out of Seattle, I anticipated a happy reunion with my old friend. I had no indication this trip would change my life.

Part of the weekend involved the ancient and sacred ritual of the sweat lodge, or the Inipi ceremony, in which the sacred Stone People are honored. The morning began with the building of a sacred fire. Kindling, larger sticks, and then bigger pieces of wood were stacked in a ceremonial way. Rocks were ceremonially placed in the wood so they would get hot when the fire burned. I learned those rocks had been specially chosen for this fire with prayers offered to the Stone People for their use in the ceremony.

The fire was lit and burning, being tended by the fire keeper. Those of us who would be participating in the lodge ceremony sat around the fire, quietly waiting for the stones to be ready. It gave me time to slow my mind, time to be still. It had been awhile since I sat outside listening to the wind, smelling the air, looking at the sky. I spent my days inside the clinic with clients. Weekends in Seattle were usually rainy. I was happy to sit on the ground and get back in touch with the earth.

Before we crawled into the dark womb of the lodge, Charla smudged each of us. She had a large abalone shell filled with sage. Taking a long match, she lit the sage, allowing it to flame. Once it was burning, she blew out the fire, leaving the plant smoldering. Curls of smoke rose up out of the shell. Using her ceremonial feather like a fan, she wafted the smoke over us, smudging us. Sage has its own sacred property: to cleanse the energy of anyone or anything who comes in contact with it. I felt honored to be purified before a ceremony in this manner. The act of smudging and ritual was new to me and yet I embraced it fully.

Readied by the smudge and Charla's instructions, we crawled into the lodge and took our places in the sacred circle sitting on the cool earth. Stones were brought in through the door and placed in a pit dug in the dirt in the center of the lodge. The door opening was covered with thick blankets. We sat in complete darkness except for the fiery red radiating off the stones. Bits of cedar were dropped onto the hot stones, releasing its fragrant and healing smell. I breathed it in. Water was poured over the glowing rocks, steam rose up, created a loud hissing sound, penetrated my body, and lifted me out of my linear consciousness.

A drum was being beat. Old, sacred songs were sung. Prayers were offered. From deep within me my prayers rose up in this sacred space, my voice joining the voices of those in the lodge with me. More water was poured onto the hot stones that sizzled loudly. The ancient ceremony transported me through time. Soft voices of ancient grandmothers whispered in my ear. The thundering of buffalo hooves striking the prairie as they ran, shaking the ground as they passed, carried me.

The smell of pure water running in wild rivers filled me. Through the intense heat of the lodge I sensed a cool, prairie wind blowing clean on my face. The vast and unencumbered night sky blazed around me, fields of stars reaching out to touch the Earth with their light. If I reached out, perhaps I could touch them . . .

Tears mingled with steam and sweat, bringing me back to my body. By the time the last water was poured, the last prayers were said, the last song sung, I knew I wanted to know more. It was time for me to explore my spiritual path in earnest. My path. I reasoned that with six billion people on the planet there were six billion ways back to God. I wanted to find my way home. The traditions of my family no longer supported me. The New Age books I avidly read and the community of people sharing those thoughts were not enough. I had to find my own spiritual identity.

The next day I had volunteered to be one of the massage therapists offering treatments to those attending the event. There were four tables set up on a large screened in porch. Getting ready to treat clients here was very much like caring for clients at home. Everything seemed normal and routine. Then, a woman named Ellen came to take her turn at my table. I asked her standard intake questions about her health status and why she wanted treatment. Ellen told me she suffered with chronic back pain and nothing seemed to help. She had come to this weekend retreat hoping for a breakthrough. Feeling that I had enough information, I waited while she stepped behind a sheet rigged up as a dressing room where she could remove her clothing for the massage. She emerged wrapped in a sheet. I helped her onto the table, adjusted the sheet around her as a drape, and made sure she was comfortable. I was focused on doing deep tissue therapy for her back.

I rubbed oil into my hands and started her massage, my open palms running down either side of her spine. As she relaxed I deepened the pressure. Suddenly, her spine looked like a large sword, the tip of which pointed past her sacrum, the hilt at the base of her neck. What was this? I had given thousands of massages and never experienced anything of this nature before. Yet, I clearly saw the sword in her back.

Even though I felt somewhat incredulous, I could not ignore this. I asked her, "Is there any reason you know of that your spine would look like a sword to me?"

She hesitated a moment and replied, "Well, yes. There is."

I was so glad I asked.

She shared some experiences she had been having recently that made her think she was reliving a past-life situation. As she told me about them the sword in her back got larger and more distinct. As she spoke, I began to have visions of her as a warrior in a great battle. She was one of hundreds, maybe thousands, of men on horseback who were charging as opposing armies spread out across a wide plain. The air was thick with dust and dirt thrown up by horses' hooves as the battle steeds galloped forward then dug in for purchase, their riders clinging to them as they clashed in personal combat. The noise was intense. Men screaming war cries and howling with the horrifying agony of deadly mayhem, sounds of horses squealing in panic, and the sickening sound of metal swords hacking through human flesh filled my ears. Putrid smells engulfed me. I was both in the vision and giving the massage at the same time, experiencing two worlds at once.

"Ellen," I asked, "do you know if this sword I am seeing has a name?"

"Yes." She spoke a name in a language I did not understand.

"Do you want me to take it out?"

"Yes, please."

And so, using my known skills as a massage practitioner and new skills that were before now completely unknown to me, I removed the sword from her back, closed up the wound, and brought her out of the battle and back to the massage table.

I was stunned.

Helping her sit up, sheet wrapped around her, I asked her how she felt. She was quiet a moment, as if assessing her body. Then, she said she felt better. Her pain was almost gone although she was very tired.

She looked at me intently and asked, "How long have you been doing this kind of work?"

"I didn't even know I did this kind of work," I replied.

I helped her get off the table so she could go get dressed. While waiting for her, I looked around the room. The other therapists were still there, each giving a massage to someone. I noticed there was soft music playing. I had been completely unaware of their existence during this amazing experience with the sword. Ellen returned from the dressing area. We stood there looking at each other, then shared a silent hug. I suggested we go outside and offer prayers for her healing and the spirit guidance that had just happened.

Years later I would come to know that what I had just done was shamanic healing.

9

An Altared Life

AS IF THE EXPERIENCES of the lodge and the shamanic healing vision were not enough, there was still one more major event in store for me before I returned to Seattle. On the same day as the sword event, we all had dinner together and, after a nice meal and conversation, reconvened out on the lawn where Charla taught a class on creating altars. There was some kind of ancient memory that awakened in me while sitting on the grass watching her build an altar. I had never really thought about altars before and found myself surprised at this omission from my life. Altars seemed basic, essential. How had I missed out on this?

Charla kept the instructions simple. Set an intention for the altar. It could be to honor your ancestors, help you find a new job, or for healing after a surgery or from an illness. Set aside a space in your home, maybe a corner of the floor or a table, to serve as the altar. Cover the top of the altar with a cloth. Set objects on the altar cloth to help hold the focus of the intention. Perhaps those objects would include candles, photographs, statues, feathers, or crystals. Take time to sit with the altar in prayer. Honor the sacred seven directions.

It was the most sensible process I had ever heard of.

By the time I left Hawkwind I was a changed woman. My spiritual quest tool bag now included the experiences of ceremony and the sweat lodge, shamanic healing, spiritual directions, and altars. All in one weekend!

When I got back to Seattle I wanted to make my own altar right away. I started with a small space on the floor against the wall between the door and my bed. It was enough out of the way where I would not step on it. The creation of it was all ritual. It felt like what I was born to do. My intention for the altar was for prayer and meditation, to remind me to take time for this every day. Making the altar was creative and joyful. I started with a small shelf board, placing it on the carpet. I found a beautiful cloth and spread it on the board, then set out special items to honor the seven spiritual directions.

West is the place of the water. I put out a small bowl filled with water on the west side of the cloth.

North is for the earth. I selected a favorite rock to honor that direction.

East is for the air. I placed a feather in a small vase opposite the bowl.

South is for the fire. A candle now faced the rock.

For the above direction I push-pinned a picture of the moon on the wall right above the altar.

I wasn't sure how to get the dimension of below on the flat surface of my altar. I thought of Gaia holding us, providing for us, how we live in such incredible beauty on our Mother Earth. I finally chose a glass heart to represent her.

That left the center, the Creator. For that I placed a beautiful, clear crystal in the center of the altar.

I smudged it all using a turkey feather.

The altar I created was now sacred space in my home.

Before crawling into bed at night I would sit in front of the altar reflecting on my day, giving thanks for the grace and goodness of my life, praying for help for myself, family, friends, and for my clients. In the morning I would give thanks for a new day. The altar became a part

The author's west altar. See the color insert, plates 2 and 3, for color photographs of the author's west and north altars.

of my life. It helped me by holding my focus. As I grew in my spiritual life, so did the altar.

It very soon became too small.

I moved the altar across the room, transforming the top of my grandmother's antique cedar chest into sacred space. I started collecting beautiful scarves and fabric to use as altar covers. All sorts of candles, candleholders, incense, matches, lighters, and even a candlesnuffer accumulated in a drawer cleaned out for altar storage. The smell of smudge permeated my condo. The new altar started sprawling across the top of the cedar chest. Pictures were push-pinned onto the walls around it. The floor on either side was becoming adorned with smaller altars, each dedicated to a purpose I wanted to bring forth in my life. Statues of Buffalo, Eagle, Coyote, Bear, and other totems of the spirit guides kept showing up in my life, moving in with me, finding a home on the altar.

Living the altared life had me walking on a tangible path I loved to follow.

Over the next two years, I kept studying the Native American wisdom shared by generous elders who had written their stories in books. I started attending women's circles, taking workshops, and attending conferences, all of which were helping me to expand my community and experiences. The offerings on my altar changed as I did, reflecting my growth. I learned about the guardians of each of the seven sacred directions, as well as how the seasons, times of the day, elements, and all aspects of life corresponded with one of these sacred gateways, or portals. My altar was becoming a crossroads to me with each direction offering a path of exploration and discovery.

One night in prayer I experienced a dramatic juxtaposition. As I sat on the floor facing the altar in front of me, I began to focus on a small ceramic figure Charla had sent to me of a woman sitting cross-legged, her open legs making the space for a tea candle to rest. Her arms were lifted up in a heart shape as her face gazed forward with a serene smile. The flickering light of the candle took over my attention. No thoughts intruded on this moment of awareness. My breath was deep and easy. The darkened room swallowed up visual distractions, hiding everything but this simple figurine. No sounds intruded into the silence growing within me. I saw only this simple goddess sitting in front of me. The light flickered, my body relaxed. I felt a shift of energy within me. The figure on the altar also shifted. She was getting larger, growing. Her arms seemed to reach out and up as she expanded her space on the altar, the light in her stone belly glowing brighter. I felt her beckon to me to come to her, to join with her. I reached out with my heart. The little statue seemed alive, breathing. I could feel her heart beating within her ceramic body. No, it was my heart beating in that porcelain form. Feeling the rhythm of life within me, I raised my arms out and above me, heart shaped above my head. My breath expanded me, lifted me. Now it was me sitting on the altar, arms upraised to Spirit, legs crossed, holding the light within me.

I had become the altar piece sitting on the altar of our Creator, occupying a sacred space in this world. I was the goddess. I was the altar. I was the light. I was the love.

10

The Elixir

BY THE TIME HURRICANE FLOYD devastated North Carolina, my altar was taking up most of one wall in my bedroom. It was while sitting on the floor in front of it, candles flickering in the otherwise dark room, that I finally heard the voice again. I was not shocked as I had been weeks ago at Greenlake. That night I accepted its presence and listened as it said:

"We want a whole room."

I knew the voice meant a whole room for the altar. Okay! No arguments from me!

"Yes, Spirit, I will do that this weekend."

Spirit replied, "We want it now!"

There was no need for me to say anything else. My response was to jump up off the floor and take immediate action! I went into the next room, which I used as my office, and started pulling out all the furniture. Fortunately for me, it was a Friday night so I did not have to get up early the next day. I stayed up all night clearing out the room. I did not know anyone who had an entire room for an altar in their home but I knew I had to do it.

Over the weekend I crammed all the trappings of the office into my bedroom. I then thoroughly cleaned and smudged the now empty room to clear all the old energy of my previous activities there. I left it sitting empty for about a week, getting the feel of all that space, allowing my intention to shift to become that of a woman with an altar room.

Finally one night, feeling the time was right, I dressed in my best ceremonial clothes and proceeded to dedicate the altar room with my intention of it being a sacred space for ceremony and prayer; a place for me to better learn how to understand and walk the spiritual path I had found. With my sage-filled abalone shell and a feather, I faced each direction, smudging that area of my room, calling in the guardians of each direction to hold open the portals to the higher knowing and protection. With the pungent scent of sage filling the room, I created an individual altar for each direction. Putting up folding tables or sturdy boxes to create a base, I covered each surface with a beautiful cloth, its color selected to match the color I had learned went with each direction. Next, I set out my altar items. Most of these pieces had already been on and around my cedar chest altar but now I could spread them out across the entire room, each finding their place in the direction they best represented. I explored my house, finding new things to include as the altars went up. Shells, crystals, feathers, old doilies crocheted by my grandmothers, little ceramic animals from my childhood, and photos all made their way into this room; each item having a special memory and purpose for the altar it became a part of. Crystal prisms hung from the ceiling next to star ornaments and a crescent-shaped moon made of blue glass. Light from the candles beneath them caused them to twinkle softly in the darkened room. A beautiful art poster of Susan Seddon Boulet's *Medicine Woman* holding a shell with smoke from her smudge wafting upwards went on the back of the door. I removed the lightbulb from the ceiling lamp. No phone, no electrical device interfered with the organic nature of this altar room.

Each wall, the ceiling, and the floor became altars, doorways, gateways, portals opening into spiritual realms I could explore.

Finally, sitting on a small rug on the floor in the center of the room, surrounded by altars, I rededicated myself to walking in this sacred way to learn all I could; to be in service, to be at one with all my relations.

Looking around at the sacred space I had created in response to the voice's direction, I felt complete; satisfied with myself.

"Spirit," I asked, "Are you happy with this?"

And the voice replied, "It's a start."

Okay, Ravenwood, stay humble!

As water needs a form to collect it, like a cup or a riverbed, so I needed a vessel to hold me in my spiritual work. For me, that vessel was my altar room. It became a sanctuary to me, my private temple; and I was keeper of the altars. I started to see myself as a ceremonialist, as a woman whose purpose was to honor Spirit in thought, action, and words. In my supplications I asked for guidance to understand the instructions I had been given by the voice at Greenlake. I realized my trust was growing: trust in myself walking farther along my spiritual path, trust in the experience of hearing the voice and following its promptings, even if it took me a few times.

The crystals I was led to find at Annie's sat in the altar room on a blue cloth on my west altar. I prayed to know what to do with them. I prayed to know how to make that crystal homeopathic elixir. I prayed for the healing of the waters in North Carolina. I started to feel like an advocate for the water.

One night, sitting in the altar room, offering my prayers, a great sense of peace and purpose came over me. I finally knew what to do.

It was time to refocus on Hurricane Floyd.

I kept mulling over the idea of water having a memory. Did the waters polluted by Hurricane Floyd remember the storm? Did the rivers, wells, groundwaters, and even the ocean hold the memory of the dead animals and toxic soup dished out by the hurricane? How long would such memories circulate through the pipes and into the bathtubs and teakettles of the South? Would that memory infect any other water that flowed into those North Carolina rivers? Did evaporated water polluted in North Carolina fall as rain in Seattle, bringing with it the cries of drowning chickens?

If the water that rinsed off the amethyst I bought at Annie's, which had flowed over my hands like liquid crystal, had memory, where did that go when it flowed down the drain of my sink? Did it wash out into Seattle's Puget Sound? Would it eventually go into the Pacific Ocean? Did my body remember it?

The answer finally came.

This time it was not from the voice giving me instructions. The answer came from inside me, a deep knowing that a truth had been revealed. It didn't come with flashes of light, drum rolls, or angels singing but rose from me having allowed a place within me to open up to and accept Spirit's directions.

Yes. I knew what to do. I would create a sacred water altar. It would be the crystal homeopathic elixir that would help to heal the waters of Gaia.

It was as if I was in the middle of a long download of information. Once started, I could not hurry it along but could only wait for more information to be revealed, trusting the process. I started with what I knew. I needed a large vessel, big enough to hold the amethyst and enough water to cover it completely. It had to be glass or a neutral material. A metal container would not work; it would rust. The element of metal was not part of the equation. A wooden bowl would be destroyed by the constant presence of water and would mold, causing the water to be affected. What to use as a container? I felt it needed to be something special and began my search.

I told my friend, Starfeather, whose monthly planetary healing circle I attended, about the whole Greenlake experience. She was very excited and supportive. She immediately thought of a wedding gift she had never used—a glass punch bowl stashed away in her garage. She retrieved it and gave it to me with her blessing. Perfect. The amethyst just fit across the bottom of the bowl.

I still did not know what purpose the mysterious wand had in all of this. No matter, just go with what I do know.

The next part of the download to be revealed for creating the sacred water altar concerned timing. It was to be synchronized with the full moon cycle. This would give the crystal about twenty-eight days of infusing its energy into the water; transforming it. Being born under the astrological sign of Cancer, which is ruled by the moon, and also being born on a full moon, this aspect was especially dear to me. Since those Wyoming summer nights sleeping in my backyard, my love of the moon was still a big part of my life. I spent many nights outside looking up at the great orb, watching her traverse her silvery path around the Earth. Her constant cycle of change from round and full to a small sliver of light fascinated me. As an avid moon watcher, I could easily synchronize myself to its schedule for the water altar.

Keeping the water altar activated, or *working the altar,* meant holding my attention on it. This was a big part of the process. In 1999 we were starting to hear more about quantum physics and how just focusing on a situation actually caused it to change. I was part of this altar. I would be part of the change. I had the choice of going forward, making a commitment to this process, or letting it pass. It was up to me. I said yes.

My nightly vigils in the altar room continued to be rewarded with more parts of the download from Spirit. The sacred water altar was to be stirred into a crystal homeopathic elixir, just as those homeopathic remedies purchased at the health-food store were created, using water and a process of stirring and reducing the ingredients until they were almost only intention. The amethyst and my prayers would act as the healing agents. The water would remember them.

Now I knew why I had to have that wand. It was to be used as the stir stick. I still did not know what kind of crystal it was. I went searching, looking around in various stores that sold crystals to see if I could discover something like my wand. I finally found a similar piece tucked into a showcase, along with a variety of other crystals for sale, at the big metaphysical store in town. Asking the clerk to show it to me, I noticed the price tag. This piece was smaller and much more expensive than the one I purchased from Annie's. Finally, that part of the mystery was solved; I now knew what that wand was. It was selenite. I had never heard of selenite and didn't know anything about it, but at least I knew what I had.

All acts begin with intention. Without that we have no focus for our desired outcome. My intention for the water altar was to make that crystal homeopathic elixir for healing Gaia's waters. On completion of the lunar cycle the water of the sacred water altar, transformed by amethyst, selenite, prayers, and intention, was to be given to the waters of the planet with prayers for healing, cleansing, and restoration.

Floyd, I think we just found your antidote.

And so, on the night of the next full moon, I set the water altar into motion. I placed the bowl, the crystals, and a jug of water on a clean cloth on the floor of the altar room. Creating a sacred space of ceremony, I began with my usual ritual, smudging myself, then the altar room—once in each direction: west, north, east, south, above, below, and center. I offered prayers of gratitude to each direction, invoking Spirit to be present. Finally, I smudged the individual components that would become the water altar: a glass punch bowl, two beautiful crystals, and a jug of water.

Placing the amethyst in the bowl, I thanked it for coming to me. I offered it my blessing and asked permission to use it for this altar. I got a deep feeling of assurance. Placing the purple beauty on the bottom of the bowl, I continued. Next I filled the bowl with water to the rim, completely covering the amethyst. I knew that the crystal would release its vibrational energy into the water, which would remember it. I had experienced the change in the water the first time I rinsed the crystal in the sink in my massage room. While I poured the water over the amethyst, I realized every point on the crystal was being activated by the water. It was as if the water and the crystal were aware of each other. The feeling was vibrant, intense, sacred. There was a kind of alchemy happening here. I felt confident that the elixir I had searched for was finally being created, tonight, in my altar room.

The voice of Spirit had become manifest in the sacred water altar.

The water in the punch bowl glowed, reflecting the candlelight in the room. The amethyst sparkled with the light. Holding the selenite wand I began to stir the water in a clockwise motion. Clockwise brings the energy in. Counterclockwise releases it. As I stirred, prayers for the water rose up out of me. I told the water I loved it. I thanked it for its life sustaining gift to all beings on the planet. I sent my love and prayers into it. As I did so, I felt the water altar send its healing remedy into me as a cool, rippling sensation. At that moment I felt myself enter into a sacred relationship with the water. This was Gaia's blood, her precious gift to us. I visualized the animals and plants that live in the water thriving; rivers running full with clean, sparkling water; and wells abundant with sweet, pure water to drink.

I visualized the Floyd-ravaged waters becoming clean and pure again.

Holding my hands over the water altar, I focused more deeply on my intention. There was nowhere else to be; nothing else to do. Time had no hold on me. Amethyst light began to shoot out of my hands into the water. Mirroring rays beamed out of the crystal, rising up into my hands, amplifying the energy. The walls of my altar room seemed to melt away. I was surrounded by a night sky dominated by the shining orb of the full moon, a silver river of light flowing from it. Like the ocean tides, I let myself be pulled along as the moon floated in the silky sky. Surrendering to her power, I watched as the sky became misted with water rising up from the Earth that glowed with a soft amethyst shimmer. The moon shone her light into the mist, illuminating the Earth's waters below with her ethereal blessing. I could hear my own voice softly resounding across the sky, amplified by the moon. My prayers joined the amethyst mist, floating across and into the Earth's lakes and oceans. They soaked into the ground through wells and aquifers. The water heard me, accepted me, drank me in.

Some time later, I felt complete. Pulling my hands back, my focus returned to the altar room. The candles had burned down almost to the ends. I had been with the water and the moon a long time.

Focusing on the altar tasks at hand, I let the selenite wand slide into the water next to the amethyst. To keep the water altar clean, I covered the bowl with a round silver platter. On top of it I placed a small fish carved from amethyst and a crab fashioned from red glass. They seemed to be appropriate as guardians of the lid. The water altar was complete. (See plates 4 and 5 for photos of the water altar.) A small table in the west end of my room became its new home; west for the waters. Feeling a great sense of peace, gratitude, and connection to something bigger than myself, I thanked Spirit for this very special night, blew out the candles, and went to bed.

11

Working the Altar

INCORPORATING THE WATER ALTAR into my life was a joyful process. My nightly ritual began with lighting all the candles in the altar room, smudging myself, and making an offering of the burning sage to each direction. These simple acts brought me relief from the stress of the day and helped me shift into a sacred time of prayer, including prayers for the water. The water altar was activated, waiting for me to do my part as the keeper of the altar. I embraced the role. I usually closed my prayer time with the water altar. Removing the silver-platter lid, I would stir the amethyst-infused water with the selenite wand. I felt my spoken words, prayers, and the energy of the crystals were being collected, amplified, and held in the water, which reciprocated by sending its cool energy rising up into my hands. It was an exchange of blessings. That connection with the water got stronger as I went along. It was feeling more like a living presence to me—like it knew what I was doing and wanted me to continue. My prayers for it were from the heart. I spoke them out loud, letting the vibration of my voice resonate into the bowl, going into the water. When finished, I would cover the bowl again.

On days that I didn't work the water altar, I found myself missing it. I was coming into a relationship not only with the altar but also into a deeper communion with the water itself, with Spirit, and with my acceptance of myself as an instrument of change. This was not something I read in a book or was taught in a workshop. This was given to me by Spirit. I was learning to listen, learning to follow the path opening in front of me. I did not know where it would lead but I had immense trust it would be to something good.

Part of following that path was to do a little more research. If I am infusing water with amethyst, stirring it with selenite, and cooking it up during a lunar cycle, just what is it I am creating in this elixir? I decided to start with the crystal piece of the puzzle. I bought a book about crystals, *Love Is in the Earth: A Kaleidoscope of Crystals* by Melody, and looked up amethyst. Many pages were dedicated to this lovely purple stone describing its physical attributes. The book also described the energetic properties of amethyst, one of which is that it "facilitates transmutation of lower energies into the higher frequencies . . . It is representative of the principles of complete metamorphisis."[1] I thought that the waters polluted by Floyd's rampaging could use some transformation! No wonder Spirit gave me an amethyst.

Now what about that selenite? It had been right there with the amethyst—the only two crystals I ever saw at Annie's. According to Melody and her book, selenite also had multiple energetic properties, but the one that resonated with me as appropriate to the water altar was its ability to "provide amelioration of disorders associated with poisoning due to the metals in the 'fillings' of teeth."[2] I thought about all the waste and poisons that were dumped into North Carolina's waterways and the water all over the world, even in our bodies. Yes, lots of poisons. The wisdom of the water altar that Spirit had entrusted to me was incredible.

Water has strong reflective power. We have all gazed into a still body of water, delighting in seeing our faces shimmering back up at us from the liquid mirror, our image surrounded by wavy trees or glimmers of light, as the water catches our surroundings and sends their images back to us. I was beginning to think that water might also collect the energy and frequency of the crystals and hold that power within its molecules.

Not only would the crystals change the water but the water would then reflect that change back out to the world.

Knowing more about the powers of the crystals helped me to better appreciate just what was happening with the water altar. My excitement about creating a Spirit-guided tool with which to actually make a difference in the world was growing. I saw no need to try to make actual homeopathic pellets (nor did I know how to do that); the atoms of the water were already functioning as carriers of the elixir's crystal properties and my prayers.

The next step in the process was in containing the elixir so I could carry it to the waters of Gaia. I started saving bottles so I would have them ready for the end of the full moon cycle. I looked at what was printed on the labels on these bottles: corporate logos, bar codes, ingredients. Remembering the beautiful exchange of energy I had experienced with the water by speaking my prayers over it, I certainly didn't want any of those corporate, commercial words being taken in by the elixir! Just as I had cleaned out the office and created the altar room in empty and purified space, I knew the elixir needed to have sacred space as well. I peeled off the labels of the empty bottles. Now there was a need for a new label. Sitting in the altar room one night, I wrote out a special prayer dedicated to the water altar and the spirit elixir created through it. These are the words that came to me:

> This water was prepared with the help of the amethyst and selenite crystals. It was stirred with the intention that one million times the energy of every crystal point be generated in healing energy and released into this water. It was stirred with the intention that it transform into a crystal, homeopathic remedy that, when released into Gaia's waters, will bring healing energy to cleanse her waters of the pollution of human miscreation: sewage, garbage, chemicals, oxygen deprivation due to overgrowth of weeds from chemicals and fertilizers, and all manner of pollution released into her waters. All water touched by this crystal homeopathic remedy will be amplified

up to one million times for each point of the crystals. This will heal all ground water, all springs, creeks, streams, rivers, and all waterways leading to the oceans. As the waters evaporate and fall again the rain, snow, sleet, and hail will be cleansed. The glaciers and snow banks will melt and run off as clean water. Each time this crystal homeopathic remedy is released it brings the power of the spirit keepers of the west, the amethyst and selenite Stone People, the power of Grandmother Moon, the intention of every prayer and stirring motion, and the love of the people who release it to cleanse Gaia's waters. And so it is.

It was a long prayer but it represented every detail of my focus with the water altar. Not wanting to second-guess myself or the ongoing creation of this altar, I accepted my lengthy prayer as part of the process. I typed out the prayer, printed copies of it onto purple paper, then cut them into my own homemade labels, taping one to each bottle. I also placed one copy of the prayer on top of the silver tray. I visualized the water taking those words into its structure, into its memory. The words became a part of the elixir: the written words, my spoken words, every word, every intention—all being absorbed into the water. It was a powerful feeling. I felt and trusted that the words were charging the water with an energy of transformation.

On the night of the next full moon, the cycle was complete. It was time to administer the elixir to Gaia. I repeated the usual smudging and ceremonial preparations. I removed the platter from the bowl and one more time stirred the water with the selenite wand, praying and blessing the water. Then, I dipped out the water, carefully pouring it into the purple-labeled bottles. With all the water emptied from the bowl, I began the process again, pouring a gallon of tap water onto the amethyst, stirring the new batch of elixir for Gaia.

I started taking these bottles with me everywhere I went, making a practice of monthly elixir offerings to Gaia. Whether it was a river, a stream, or one of the nearby lakes or beaches, being with the water put me into a ceremonial frame of mind. It was a sacred time of prayer and gratitude; like being in my altar room. I liked to just sit and listen to the water as it flowed and moved. Its cadence seemed to resonate in my body making me feel fluid and reflective. Not only could I see my own reflection in the water but also the reflection of all life around it; the trees growing along the water's edge, birds flying by, the clouds above me. Sometimes raindrops fell, making little splashes on the water's surface, drumming a fluid rhythm. I came to have a deeper appreciation of the plants, animals, and conditions around the different bodies of water I visited. It was a time to be in relationship with the water, with the earth around me, with Gaia.

Sitting at the edge of a stream, on a stone out in a river, or wading out along a beach, I would open the bottles of the elixir and begin my prayers, gradually pouring out the contents of the bottles, watching the elixir blend with the living, flowing water. I imagined the purple of the amethyst spreading out through each drop of water, carrying its homeopathic remedy of the crystals along with my love and healing intentions to the waters. I visualized the fish and plants drinking up this elixir, receiving the intentions I had stirred into it. I imagined it finding its way to North Carolina, replacing memories of chicken carcasses with beautiful amethyst energy; transforming poisons into purity.

One day a song came to me as part of the blessing. "Thank you, Water. Bless you, Water. Thank you Water." I began to sing this simple, lilting chant along with my prayers each time I worked the water altar or released the elixir.

The more I worked with the sacred water altar, the more I came to know and understand that making an offering in one body of water affected all water. I did not have scientific proof of this. But it made sense to me. My spiritual practice supported that we are all one. We are Gaia's children, all part of that sacred hoop. All beings are related. The trees, known as the Standing People, and the crystals, known as the Stone People, all are connected, connected to each other, connected to us as humans. What happens for one happens for all. Certainly the backlash of Floyd had been felt far from the original site of washed-out collection lagoons full of animal waste materials. Even a year later, bodies of pigs were being pulled out of the North Carolina wetlands; their rotting carcasses a continual source of contamination to the water and all who depend on it for life. The flood of waste had swept out into the ocean where all the creatures who came in contact with it would breathe it into their gills, absorb it through their skin, and in their food. In turn, those fish were consumed by humans who then took the Floyd factor into their own bodies.

Floyd had affected me, way up in the Puget Sound area of the Pacific Northwest, and had caused me to connect with Spirit and go beyond the boundaries of my current life. That hurricane caused the sacred water altar to be created and all the subsequent prayers I might never have uttered otherwise.

I started to share the purple-prayer-labeled bottles with my friends, instructing them in how to make prayers for the healing of Gaia's waters. At that point in time we could still board airplanes carrying our own water. Friends flew with one or two bottles, taking them along on their trips. One friend took hers to Hawaii and released it while swimming with dolphins. The water went all over Washington state and Oregon to the ocean, rivers, lakes, and backyard ponds. Anytime I went on any trip, long or short, I took it with me.

12

Journey

The Crystal Cave

◎ Intention

Our intention for this journey is to visit a crystal cave deep in the earth where you will be given tools to use in your sacred water altar.

Bring your attention to your breath. Inhale. Exhale. Feel your body relax. Imagine you are sitting comfortably over a small opening into the earth. Inhale. Expand your ribs, filling your lungs. Exhale. Send that breath down and out of your body into the earth below you. Inhale. Draw your breath up from the earth, into your body. Your breath is enriched from the earth below. Your mind relaxes and tensions drop away.

Inhale again, deeper this time, feeling the earth energy filling your heart chakra. Exhale. Send your out-breath back to the earth. With each cycle of breath you feel more connected to the earth below you. Your body is naturally giving in to be held in this comforting energy. Breathe in. Exhale. Allow your senses to connect with the earth; the rich soil beneath you, the rocks, and tree roots. The ground feels cool away from the sun's light. You feel safe, secure. Go deeper into the earth. Draw in the power of the earth.

You become aware of a sound deep in the earth—a steady rhythm—like a drum beat. You feel this rhythm in your body. You feel it in your heart. Your heart entrains to this rhythm. You are in sync with it. It is the heartbeat of Mother Earth. Follow this heartbeat deep into the earth.

You are walking now along an underground path spiraling downward, following the heartbeat sound. You feel a deep longing to connect with that heartbeat. What is it like to walk below the surface? Are you barefooted? What are you wearing? Notice the path, how it feels beneath your feet. It is not dark here. The path glows with a pale light. You realize the light is coming from the ground itself.

You reach the end of the path and find yourself in a very large cave. You step off the path and onto the floor of the cave. The ground is somewhat sandy and feels damp under your feet. You can hear the sound of water dripping. Looking up you see beautiful stalactites hanging from the ceiling of the cave. In places, stalagmites grow upward from the floor toward the formations above. A glowing light illuminates these structures making them look like vertical rainbows.

You begin to walk deeper into the cave. The air smells incredibly fresh and clean; pristine. The sounds of water are all around you. You hear it dripping from the cave ceiling. You hear it gurgling; flowing. Follow the sound of the water. You can smell the water. What does it smell like to you? The oxygen in the cave carried by the water makes you feel invigorated; clean. You breathe in deeply, absorbing its beneficial energy as you walk in the cave.

You are now at the center of the cave where a crystal clear spring of water rises up from the earth. It creates a pool of pure water. You walk up to the pool, kneel down, and place your hands in this pristine water. What does the water feel like? What does it smell like? Can you hear it? See it? You cup your hands, lifting the water to your mouth to drink. Drink the water. Feel the water as it passes your lips, into your mouth, and down your throat. Every cell in your body is alerted and opens itself to receive this precious gift. Feel the water move through your cells. Feel the water become a part of you.

As you drink, you notice that the pool is lined with crystals; amethyst crystals. You look around and realize that the entire cave is formed from amethyst. The cave is glowing with a purple light in hues from deep purple-black to pale lavender. Notice how beautiful they are. Feel the power of the amethyst vibrate through your body; your consciousness. Allow the vibration of the crystals to resonate throughout your consciousness.

The water is also aglow with the purple color of the amethyst. It hums as if it is singing. Take another drink of the water. Feel the color move through you. Feel the frequency of the amethyst humming through your body; singing inside you.

Other types of crystals also grow in this cave. You begin to notice the different layers or bands of colors interspersed with the amethyst. One particular crystal gleams and captures your attention. What is this crystal that is calling out to you? Perhaps it is amethyst or some other crystal. Pick it up. Look at it. The crystal is formed into a beautiful vial. It is a truly amazing piece. Notice the shape of the vial, its texture, its color. How does it feel in your hand? What does it look like? What is the vibration of it?

The vial is a gift to you from the cave, from the water. The water wants to go with you. Fill the vial with the water from the pool. Hold the vial up and look at the water now inside it. Feel its vibration. Can you hear it humming? Is it speaking to you? Listen.

You notice there is a small lid attached to the vial with a chain of crystal beads. You attach the lid to the vial and hang the vial around your neck, letting it rest against your body. You can feel the crystal and water vibrating against your body. You feel the vibrations enter into your body. You feel them just as you felt the water you drank move through your mouth and throat into your cells.

Take another drink from the pool. Put your mouth into the water and drink it in. Feel it hydrate you, refresh you, nourish you. Lean forward closer to the water . . . closer . . . until you simply slip into the water. Now you are immersed in the pure, amethyst water. What does it feel like? Notice how your body is completely relaxed. Your mind is at ease. Your heart is wide-open, receiving this water, receiving the energy of the crystals.

Now the water begins to move you out of the stillness of the pool. Perhaps it bubbles around you. Feel the water gently moving you. It propels you through its peaceful, liquid body. You feel yourself moving along the course of the water, starting as a stream, becoming wider until you are floating in an underground river. The river is vast, wide, deep. It is a great river flowing through this cave and you are gently carried along with it, in it. How does it feel to be here? Allow yourself to float free. Listen to the water. What is it telling you? What do you see as you flow with it?

The pace of the river speeds up. You are moving along faster and can feel the increased power of the water. The river is flowing uphill now, coming closer to the roof of the cave. The light increases and you notice shafts of it breaking through the cave ceiling. When the light shines on the water it sparkles like crystals. Absorb this liquid light. Let it glow within each of your cells. Drink it in.

The sound of the river is strong as it pushes itself upward and forward. Listen to the river. The light is brighter and you can see an opening in the ground above you. The water follows the light, flowing upward, lifting you up toward it, carrying you as it flows up—out of the cave and into the sunlight. Feel the sunlight warming your body. It is as if you have never seen the sun or felt it on your skin before. Enjoy the warmth of the sun.

As the water carries you out of the cave, you experience a wonderful feeling. You feel you have been reborn; as if the water has given birth to you. How does it feel to you now to be renewed by the water, re-emerging into the light?

You continue to float in the river as it follows its course downstream. You see life all around you. Trees line the river banks. Flowers and plants grow along each side. Birds fly overhead in a beautiful blue sky. The water gives life to all beings—plants, animals, humans. Notice the life around you. You find other creatures are in the water with you, sharing this watery ride with you—fishes, animals, plants. Who is sharing this journey with you?

The river curves and bends. It slows down, gracefully meandering along its path. You are gently pulled out of the main current into a deep pool near the bank of the river. You float peacefully in this pool. How is it to float in this pool? Notice how you feel. Perhaps the water is telling you something. A guide is there for you. The guide has come to offer a message to you. What does the guide tell you? What does the guide show you? Enjoy your time in the pool. Enjoy this time with your guide.

Now it is time to get out of the water. You draw yourself up and onto the soft grass growing here. Warm sunlight dries your body. As if you were expected, you find dry robes to put on and wrap yourself in them. Your hand goes to the crystal vial around your neck. You gently cup it, feeling the vibrations coming from it, feeling your own *vibration in sync with the crystal. Hold the vial full of the water and feel its power. This crystal vial will always keep you connected with the pure source of water from the crystal cave. You realize that the crystal cave water you drank is also part of you. You can still feel it moving within you.*

You have received great gifts from the cave, from the water, from the crystals and your guide. You want to give a gift in return. Put your hand into your robe pocket. There is something there that you will offer back to the water. What will you give to the water? Step back into the pool and make your offering now. The waters bubble up around you, pulling your offering down into its depths, accepting your gift.

Allow yourself a few moments to commune with the water. Ask anything you want of it. Listen to what it might say to you; what it might ask of you. Feel whatever message it may have for your body. Drink it in. Feel it circulate through every cell. You are connected now with this water forever. It is a part of you. You are a part of it.

You return to the grassy ground and rest. Notice your breath. As you breathe in, you can feel the amethyst energy vibrating inside of you. You exhale and the river seems to take away your breath to recycle it back into the molecules of the river. Breathe in. Breathe out. Feel the ground beneath you. Feel your breath transport you back into this present time and space. Feel the crystal vial around your neck and know you bring it back with you.

And now, you are back from your journey.

Deepening Your Practice

In this journey, the amethyst cave and its pure water offered a gift of a crystal vial. You were invited to fill the crystal vial with the water from the amethyst pool to take with you. If you accepted these gifts, you can include in your sacred water altar a piece of whatever crystal the vial was made from. For instance, if your vial was made from rose quartz, then include a piece of that into the vessel holding your water altar or use it as a stirring wand. You might also benefit from deeper study of the values of whatever crystal you were given in the journey.

When you create your water altar, and anytime you pray with it, shift your consciousness and return to the place of the crystal cave. Recall the vial and water, and include that etheric water into your physical water altar. If a guide gave you special teachings, include those in your prayers at the water altar. When you release the elixir from your altar out into the waters of Gaia, visualize that pure, amethyst cave water, which is the archetypal energy of the earth's pristine water, flowing out into the polluted waters of our earth to help restore purity to the water.

13

Creating Your
Sacred Water Altar

AN ALTAR IS A COSMIC DOORWAY—a portal that opens to other dimensions. The prayers and meditations we offer at the altar go out through the portal. The manifestation of our altar returns to us through that same portal. Creating an altar is not unlike planting seeds in a field. With care and nurturing your altar, what you planted grows and manifests. Your water altar will spring up out of that field of possibility and Spirit will flow into your life. It is most important to set your clear intention for what you want your altar to be. Unlimited potential provides for unlimited altars! However, as the voice directed me to make a crystal homeopathic elixir to heal the waters of Gaia, then that shall be our intention here.

Quantum physics has clearly shown that our intentions, focus, and actions do change or alter the energy to the purpose of our focus. Whenever you sit at your altar in meditation or prayer, the energy and dedication you give it are enhanced by the intention you have infused into the altar. Creating an altar creates a power spot—a place of purpose where your intention and connection to the divine are amplified. Altars will continue to hold your intention and energy even when you are not working them. Even the most simple of altars does this. Most people already have one in their kitchen: it is the door of the refrigerator, covered with photos of loved ones or magnets purchased on a vacation. Every time the attention is placed back on that decorated door, we relive the moments and emotions captured in the pictures or in the memories of our trip. We stay connected through the refrigerator altar.

To create your sacred water altar, spend some time meditating; thinking of or visualizing all the ways that water manifests in life. Think of the many ways you depend on water each day, how you cannot live without it. Dedicate the water altar you are about to create with the intention of it becoming a crystal homeopathic elixir that heals the waters of Gaia. This is real. It works. You are creating a healing altar of which you become the guardian and keeper. You are a priestess or priest of the waters and this altar is your temple. The energy, ceremony, ritual, and attention you pour into your sacred water altar will increase its potency. Ritual and ceremony are always enhanced by the tools used. Choose your tools with intention and gratitude. You are creating a doorway into the sacred. The more you walk through that doorway, the more proficient you will become at it and the deeper your relationship will be to Water and to Spirit.

Deepening Your Practice

Water has many qualities. As you prepare to create your sacred water altar, think of the many properties of water. Here are just a few.

Water:

    is a conductor of energy;

    is reflective;

    is a universal solvent;

    flows;

    soothes;

has memory;

cleans;

supports all life—nothing can live without it;

hydrates;

takes the shape of whatever it is contained in;

transforms from liquid, to solid, to gas;

holds a baby afloat in the womb;

forms rivers, oceans, streams, wells, springs, ponds,
pools, and lakes;

manifests as rain, snow, sleet, hail, fog, mist, and ice;

combines with the other elements;

erodes;

is a carrier—it holds what is put into it;

manifests in the body as tears, body fluids, blood,
cerebral spinal fluid, plasma, and saliva.

As you go about your day, bring your attention more to water. The above list is small and general. Increase your awareness of the specific ways water moves through your life and your relationship with water.

DEDICATED SPACE

First, set your intention that your sacred water altar will help bring you into a deeper relationship with the water. Its combined purpose is to create a crystal homeopathic elixir to heal the waters, as a place for prayer and meditation, and to be a doorway through which to explore sacred realms. As you work your altar with your prayers and intentions, it will be a portal for blessings and inspirations to be poured back onto you, and into the waters of Gaia. When you feel your intention is fully set, it is time to create your sacred water altar.

Select a permanent place for the water altar. In spiritual

traditions, each physical direction, north, south, east, west, is home to an element. Water is traditionally associated with the west so, if possible, choose a location in the west region of your home for the water altar. It does not have to be a large space, but it needs to be dedicated to the altar. The water altar is a permanent creation until you consciously decide you no longer want to maintain it. You will not be moving it, taking it apart, or using its components for other purposes. It is important to choose a place that will accommodate that intention. The top of your TV or bookshelf is not recommended. Size is not really important, use what is available to you. A small table works best, but you can use the floor if you do not have any other good option. If you do use the floor and it is covered in carpeting, remember that carpeting is not level and will not make a stable base for the water altar. Put something flat down on top of the carpet to create a base; perhaps heavy cardboard, a metal cookie sheet or pizza pan, a shelf board, or a thin piece of lumber. If you have wood floors, you might want to protect them from any possible drips as you work your water altar.

If possible, choose a private place in your home so you can sit with the water altar undisturbed and where it will not be in the way of household traffic. If you are sharing the altar with other people, you will all need to create this together, along with your communal intention. If you share a household and only you will be working this altar, it is important to educate your family or housemates so that your privacy and the sacredness of the altar are respected.

Once you choose a space, clean it. Vacuum the rug, sweep and wash the floor, wash the walls and windows around it. You are creating a sacred space for Spirit to visit you. Clean with nontoxic chemicals; be aware of what you put into the water. There are a variety of excellent green cleaners to choose from. If you are using a table or some other furniture for the water altar base, clean it as well. If it is a dresser, empty the drawers. You can use them to store your altar needs, journal, or items you collect as you work your altar.

SMUDGING

When everything is clean, the base for the altar is assembled, and you are ready to go forward, smudge the entire area of the altar and everything you will be using on it. Smudging is an ancient ritual of purification. You may already know how to smudge and use it in your life. If you are not acquainted with the process, this is how it works. First, acquire sage. This is not the garden-variety herb, but the kind that grows as sagebrush across the western plains or another popular variety called California white sage. Either sage is fine and is usually readily available at metaphysical or herb stores. You might find them for sale at a booth at a music festival or farmers' market, or down the incense aisle of an organic grocery store.

If using a smudge stick, which is sage tied into a bundle, be sure to hold it over some kind of container to catch any ashes that may drop. A traditional container is an abalone shell. Sage bundles are often sold with one of these shells. However, you can use any kind of heatproof container. Some people use a very small cast iron skillet (the model size), or a metal pan with a handle, or even a large ashtray. Whatever you use, it needs to be clean, free of advertising slogans, and something you can leave with the altar. It will be dedicated to your smudging ritual so it must be something you don't need to use for other purposes.

You might also smudge with cedar, another cleansing plant. The rich oil in the cedar burns hot and tends to pop so be very careful if you use it. Many smudge bundles contain a combination of sage, cedar, and even lavender.

Lay the pieces of sage or the smudge stick in the container. Light the sage and let it flame. You can use a match or lighter. Seasoned smudgers often call their altar lighter the sacred Bic. Then, blow out the flame (be careful not to blow ashes across the room) and let the sage smolder. First, hold your hands over the smoke to purify your own energy. Then, using a feather or your hand, waft the smoke across your body, front and back, to fully clear yourself. Don't forget your feet. Next, smudge your altar area, sending the smoke over each direction of the altar and over all the objects you use on it. It is best to open a window or door to allow the smoke to clear and take the stagnant or negative energy with it. This act of purification is best repeated each time you visit your altar.

Some people are adversely affected by smoke and cannot tolerate smudging. If this is true for you, or your housemates or pets, you can use sage or cedar without lighting it; performing etheric smudging where you would simply visualize the energy clearing you and your altar space. Remember that intention is as powerful as the flame that burns your sage.

After you have smudged the area, you may extinguish any remaining smoldering pieces. I use a flat rock to gently crush out the fire. I leave this rock in my smudging shell and it is not used for any other purpose. Or, you might choose to let the sage burn all the way out while you say your prayers and work your altar. Be sure the bottom of your smudge shell or pan is not so hot it burns or scorches where it sits. As a precaution, I set my smudge shell on a slab of rock. I have burned through more than one abalone shell over the years. Fire is persistent.

Harvesting Your Own Sage and Creating Smudge Sticks

If you live in an area where sage grows, the mindful harvest of live plants can be a wonderful field trip with Spirit. Your day is spent focused on gathering the sage to help you in your ceremonies. Usually you have to drive away from the city and so experience a beautiful day in nature. Be sure not to harvest from private land without permission. Don't drive out over the land: stay on roads. Be respectful of the environment.

When you approach a plant, offer it some tobacco, water, or other honoring gift. Give thanks for its life and ask the plant spirits if they are willing to have you harvest from this plant. If you feel you may proceed, do not take too much from any one plant. Use garden-sized pruning shears. Cut from the leafy part of the plant as thicker stems will be more difficult to burn when you smudge. Cuttings are ideally around 6–12 inches. Collect the cuttings onto a sheet or basket. When you have gathered a good supply, offer your thanks again to the plants and leave.

To prepare the smudge sticks, gather up pieces of sage into a bundle about 1–2 inches thick. These will end up being mostly cylindrical, with the stems at the bottom and the leafy ends on top. They may be slightly damp from the oil in the sage. Using cotton thread (it burns more cleanly) tie the bundles securely so the pieces do not fall out but not so tight as to restrict the flow of air through the bundle. You want an even burn through the sage. Start at the bottom, wrapping the thread several times around the stems. Then make spiral wraps up the leaves and back down again, securing the thread into a knot at the stems. You can use any color of thread that appeals to you or you might select specific colors that remind you of the water. Your smudge sticks might be damp with oil after you wrap them. If so, let them dry for a few days; stacking them loosely to allow air to move around them. I recommend tying your bundles as soon after collecting the sage as possible. Dry sage is brittle and more difficult to wrap.

Cedar: If you are using cedar in your bundles, follow the same protocol. Remember you are harvesting from live trees. Take from the lower branches and cleanly cut the pieces you take. Do not strip away bark. Cedar becomes very brittle when it dries so be sure to tie it into your bundles before that happens.

Lavender: If using lavender, collect the flower stalks and dry them first before adding to a smudge bundle. Fresh lavender does not burn well. You might grow your own lavender or ask friends or neighbors if you can harvest from their plants.

Whatever plants you choose, please use all you take. Do not waste this precious resource.

You can layer the sage, cedar, and lavender as you wrap your bundles. Sage burns the best of the three so try to make it the primary ingredient. Please remember that by burning the sage you will be introducing fire to whatever environment you are in. Be safe, use caution, and always have a container for your smudge and a way to extinguish it.

FEATHERS

Feathers are a standard part of ritual and altars. They represent the element of air. Wafting smoke with a feather is efficient, easier than using your hand, and lends a certain elegance to ritual. Any feather you use holds the energy of the bird it came from. It is important to honor that bird that gave away its feather to you. Keep feathers off the ground. Some people keep theirs in a special box where the feathers are protected. Some gently wrap them in red cloth, honoring them as sacred. If you have the skill, you can bead the quill of the feather or wrap it in leather, decorating that with crystals or other special items. You can use a single feather, or create a fan using multiple feathers, or even the entire wing. Feathers can also be dyed or painted.

Please know that certain feathers are illegal to possess, such as eagle, condor, hawk, and other protected birds. A turkey feather is legal and is commonly used in rituals as it is large enough to be effective and represents abundance and sharing. Its energy is often called the *giveaway* and it reminds us that Spirit gives all of life to us and we give back our love and gratitude to the resources that sustain us.

Use of feathers is a personal choice. They are not essential to the sacred water altar.

COMPONENTS OF
YOUR SACRED WATER ALTAR

The Altar Cloth

Your water altar will be covered with a cloth to create a base for the altar items that will sit on top of it. Choosing an altar cloth can be fun as well as full of intention. Perhaps you choose a cloth that has the colors of the ocean or one that appeals to your sense of beauty. My mother passed on to me many lovely linens embroidered or crocheted by my grandmothers. I like to use these family treasures for my altar cloths. Serendipity happens so you might be surprised with a gift of just the perfect cloth at the perfect time. If your budget allows, you might prefer to go shopping for your altar cloth. Whatever you choose, it will be dedicated to your water altar and not used for any other purpose. Be sure the cloth is clean. You might need to iron it. The surface needs to be smooth so you can set other things on top of it. Lay it out over the top of your table or onto the floor. An added benefit of a nice altar cloth is that it hides what it sits on. This allows you to create your altar from something that might not be visually appealing but is sturdy and useful.

The Vessel

The next item for the water altar is the vessel that will hold the water. I use a glass punch bowl that holds about a gallon of water. Use glass, ceramic, or stone. I like to see the water inside the bowl so clear glass is preferable for me. A metal bowl will rust, a wooden one will swell and get moldy. Do not use plastic as the chemicals in plastic will leach into the water. The bowl you choose is now dedicated to the water altar and will not be used for any other purpose. Thrift stores have an abundance of suitable bowls if you don't have anything at home to use. You don't have to spend a lot of money to create this altar but your intention is priceless. The vessel is best matched in size to hold the crystals you are going to use. If the crystals fill the entire bowl there will not be room for water or for stirring the water. You can make this water altar big or small. It just depends on your crystals, how much room you have, and how big of an altar you want to maintain.

The Lid

Since water evaporates, you will want to keep a lid on the bowl. This also prevents any debris from falling into it. I use a round, silver tray I received long ago as a wedding present. If you use a cloth to cover the bowl, be sure it is large enough to really drape the bowl and anchor the cloth so it is unlikely to fall down into the water. I prefer a solid lid. It sits securely over the water, protecting it, and I can use it as an extension of the water altar. I keep my stirring wand of selenite on the lid, as well as a photo of me giving the water to the ocean, a glass crab, and a written prayer for the water. My water altar is surrounded with large selenite slabs but that is an optional enhancement.

The Dipper

When it is time to remove the water from the vessel and transfer it into your specially prepared bottles, you will need some kind of dipper. A glass measuring cup with a spout works well. You might choose a soup ladle or a special cup. A funnel is also useful to keep spills at a minimum. Whatever you decide to use, keep the dipper with your altar, not using it for other purposes.

Your Crystals

Spirit gave me amethyst for the water altar base and selenite to stir with. I recommend you use these same components. They are readily available, fairly inexpensive, and come in a wide variety of sizes. Size is not crucial but larger crystals have more crystal points to amplify their frequencies and so generate more energy. However, some smaller crystals can be very potent. After you have made a relationship with your water altar you might discover other crystals are more appropriate for you, but since this is what the voice led me to, these are the crystals used in this teaching. Crystals are alive. They are also referred to as the sacred Stone People. They give away their individual vibrational frequencies, their light, color, and healing qualities to help restore and maintain balance to the world. Remember that the specific characteristics of these crystals will be infused into the water as part of the crystal homeopathic elixir to heal the waters of Gaia.

Your intention is very powerful in this water altar. Let Spirit assist you. This is more about your relationship with the water, Spirit, and your sacred water altar, than details. If amethyst and selenite are not available, you might consider rose quartz, for compassion and love, or a clear quartz, for clarity and purity. This is a lot like making a cup of tea. You start with water and infuse a tea bag or tea leaves into the water. The water then takes on the character of the plant; what was plain water is now peppermint, or licorice, or chamomile tea—a blend of the water and the plant properties. When you drink the tea you are drinking in all the benefits of the water, which has become the carrier that brings the benefits of the plant to you. The water is changed and as you drink the tea, those changes enter into you, interacting with the water in your cells, changing you. The same is true with the crystals and water. Different crystals have different qualities. If you choose a crystal other than what is discussed in this book, please research it first to understand what properties it offers.

If you do not have crystals, and cannot afford to purchase any, improvise. Ask Spirit to guide you in your choice. You might use a stone from a river or the ocean. The purpose of the crystals is to hold the work of the water altar within them, magnifying their energy into the water, carrying your intention, and sharing their healing frequency with the water to create the alchemy—the elixir—to transform the water to a higher level of purity.

Programming Your Crystals

Like the other components of your water altar, the crystals you use will be dedicated to it and not be used for any other purpose. If you already have a relationship with crystals, you will know to communicate with them regarding their agreement to work with you in the water altar. For those of you unfamiliar, this is a basic element in being in relationship with the Stone People. Just as we would ask permission to borrow and use something belonging to a friend, we ask the Stone People if they are willing to do this work with us. Communicating with your crystals is part of coming into a deeper awareness of the world we live in. Spend some time getting to know your crystals. Hold them. What do they feel like? How do you feel when you hold them? Are you able to detect an energy shift within yourself when you are with them? Sleep with them; dream with them. Notice any feelings of being connected with them.

Program your crystals. This is a simple but important process. After you have selected the crystals for your water altar, cleanse them with clean water, removing all dirt and debris. You can use your sink, a creek or river, or the ocean. While you are doing this, ask the crystals if they are willing to be the base of your sacred water altar. Tell them your intention of the water altar and how you need their help. Listen to hear if they have any response to you. You might register any response as audible, as a feeling, through a dream, or just a knowing. Trust your own process.

After cleansing them, let them sit in the sun to dry. If you leave them outside choose a safe place where people and animals will not disturb them. Or leave them on a sunny window ledge. I like to set mine outside in my Medicine Wheel, allowing them a full day of sunshine, and leave them there overnight under a full moon.

When you feel you are ready to proceed, program your crystals for the sacred water altar. Smudge yourself and the crystals. Give thanks to the Stone People for their giveaway to you and to this water altar. Thank them for coming into your life and being in service to your altar. Hold the crystal and speak into it, stating your intention for using it. You may want to write this out before your ceremony or just speak from your heart. You are infusing your intention into the crystal, which will hold that intention within its crystalline structure. When the water interacts with it, the crystal releases its own quality as well as your stored intention into the water. The memory of the water then carries those qualities within its cells. Repeat the process with all crystals used in your sacred water altar.

An amazing thing happened over time with my altar. Every time I prayed with the water altar, I used that first wand of selenite found in Annie's antique store to stir the water in the bowl. When I was done, I would leave the selenite wand in the water, resting on top of the amethyst. After a few months, the wand seemed smaller to me. At first I thought I just imagined it, but then realized it actually was diminishing in size. The selenite was slowly melting into the water! It was a complete giveaway of the crystal to the water. I eventually put that wand into the water with the amethyst. I bought a new selenite wand for stirring and kept it on the lid between uses.

This was a very humbling realization for me of the total giveaway of the selenite to the water altar. It brought me deeper into gratitude for the service of the Stone People.

Since so much of my water altar work has been related to the moon, it is not surprising that selenite showed up for me. The Greek name for the goddess of the moon is Selene—just one more connection to the lunar energy of the water altar.

PUTTING IT
ALL TOGETHER:
THE FULL MOON CYCLE

The altar is created, the components gathered, the crystals programmed. Now it is time to assemble all the parts. Spirit told me the sacred water altar was to be kept from full moon to full moon. Using this moon cycle allows the crystals time to infuse their energy into the water and for you to come into a relationship with the process. The more you sit with your water altar, pray with it, and stir the waters in it, the deeper your relationship with it becomes. Daily prayer is optimal but do the best you can. Think of time with your water altar as a date with Spirit. The more time you spend on these dates the more you will get to know Spirit and your water altar.

If you find that the full moon cycle does not resonate with you, pray and ask Spirit to reveal a plan best for you.

ACTIVATION

It is time to activate this altar. Smudge. Prepare yourself for a time to be with Spirit. You might choose to use a candle on your altar. If you do, keep the flame clear of any curtains or flammable items. Light the candle when you are at the altar and extinguish it when you leave. Or use a battery-operated candle if you cannot tolerate candle smoke or do not want flames in your home. These candles are readily available at many stores.

Place the programmed amethyst (or main crystal) in the bottom of your bowl. Keep offering your prayers for your intention of the water altar, for the healing of the waters. Visualize your efforts making a difference for clean and pure water. Visualize the water restored.

Pour water over the amethyst. Fill the bowl almost to the top, leaving only enough room to stir without spilling over the sides. Then take your crystal wand and begin to stir the waters clockwise (to bring in the energy) while speaking your prayers directly over the water. Visualize your words going into the water and becoming a part of its memory. Visualize the crystals releasing their energy into the water. Visualize this water becoming a crystal homeopathic elixir to heal the waters of Gaia. Stir all of this into the water. Know that your words change the frequency of the water just as the crystals' frequency does. You can read a prayer you have written out and rehearsed or just offer what comes from your heart. Ask the crystals to give themselves fully to the task. Ask the water to receive the gifts being offered it. You are indeed creating an elixir that will heal the waters of Gaia when released. Don't hold back! Pour your heartfelt effort into the water.

Believe this. What you are speaking creates change. Tell the water you love it. Say thank you. Visualize the water of your sacred water altar becoming a powerful potion. "Thank you, Water, for your gift of life. I see you clean and restored. Thank you, Water, bless you Water."

In time perhaps, as you pray you might actually see the words as they come out of your mouth. Yes, words are tangible. We don't think about this as we speak, sometimes rattling on about nothing, but it is true. Prayers at your water altar are incredibly powerful. Learn to watch your words.

When you feel complete, stop. You may leave the wand in the bowl resting on the amethyst or rest it on the altar, perhaps on the lid. Cover the bowl with the lid.

Return to the water altar often during the month. Incorporate this altar into your life.

CONTAINERS TO HOLD THE ELIXIR

You will need bottles or jars to transport the elixir from the sacred water altar to the living waters of Gaia for ceremony. During the month you can start to collect these. Be sure any container you use is clean and free of odors from its previous occupant. Remove any commercial bar codes and labels. The containers need to have tightly fitting lids. Whatever the volume of water in your water altar, you will need enough containers to hold that same amount. You can put it all into one container or divide the elixir into smaller containers. This is what I do. It makes for easier transport and also for sharing with friends. Like the bowl, glass is best, metal will rust, and wood will mold. While I would not use plastic for the water altar bowl, I do use plastic bottles to transport the elixir out into the world. They are lightweight and will not break, so they are easy to carry. As the elixir is usually only in them for a few hours there is not much time for the chemicals from the plastic to leach out. Besides, the elixir can help to counteract the plastic elements. If you don't buy water or other drinks that come in plastic bottles you can ask people to save theirs for you. Glass jars or bottles are excellent, preferable to use, but they are breakable. Remember you will be out in nature. If you carry glass with you try not to drop and break it.

Plate 1. Deep blue waters
in the Hoh Rain Forest,
Washington

Plate 2 (above). West and north altars of the author's altar room

Plate 3 (below). Detail of the author's west altar

Plate 4. The author's water altar: glass bowl, amethyst, selenite wand, and sacred water

Plate 5. The water altar covered with a silver platter (to keep it clean), watched over by an amethyst fish and glass crab

Plate 6. The author
in her altar room

Plate 7. Smudging the altar
area for purification

(Plates 5 through 8
photos by Nancy Roy.)

Plate 8. Stirring the water
with the selenite wand

Plate 9. Giving the water elixir
to Gaia.

Plate 10. Thoth at the
Temple of Seti I in Abydos, Egypt

Plate 11. Sunrise at Aswan, Egypt

Plate 12. The author prepares for her lineage transmission ceremony with Nicki Scully on Elephantine Island, Egypt.

Plate 13. Nicki weaves the ancient
lineage transmission ceremony.

Plate 14. Amethyst-colored
water at the edge of the Nile,
following the ceremony
on Elephantine Island

Plate 15. The beautiful
columns of the outer
courtyard at
the Temple of Isis
at Philae

Plate 16. The Temple of Isis,
Philae

LABELS

Prepare a label for every container that will hold the sacred water altar elixir. This can be a fun and creative process. I use purple paper (purple for the amethyst) and print a prayer for the water onto it. Your labels represent your intention for the water. You can write out words of love and gratitude; create label art with your favorite medium; or cut out pictures from magazines that specifically show water in loving, pure, and beautiful ways; or pictures showing the beauty of Gaia. Remember that whatever is on the label will energetically enter into the water inside the container.

After your labels are created, wrap one around each container, taping it into place. I suggest you reuse these containers, so making the label watertight is a good idea. If you don't want plastic tape in the equation, just write or draw directly onto the container. Of course, you can create new labels as often as you like.

Keep your containers with your altar. I have a cloth bag I use just for this purpose and keep that next to the altar. I never have to go searching for something to use when it is time to take the elixir to Gaia. These containers are not used for anything else. They are part of the sacred water altar.

COMPLETING THE CYCLE

At the next full moon you will complete the cycle. The water altar has had a month to build the potency from the crystals and your prayers into a powerful elixir. Set your date with Spirit. When the time arrives, prepare yourself for ceremony. Smudge yourself and the altar area. Remove the lid and one more time stir the water clockwise as you repeat your prayers. Thank the water altar for holding the energy for this past month. Thank the moon, your guides, and Spirit for this work.

Using the dipper you have for the water altar, start to remove the water from the bowl pouring it into the prepared containers with your labels. I like to remove the bowl from the altar, setting it on a towel to soak up any drips or spills that might occur. As you fill each container, feel the excitement of the creation of this elixir! The water has been transformed. You have been an agent of alchemy! Each drop is now a precious, transforming elixir for the waters of Gaia.

After all the water has been poured into your containers, you are ready to begin the cycle again. If you removed the bowl from the altar, put it back. Pour the new supply of water over the amethyst and stir your intentions and prayers into it. When you are complete, cover it with the lid. Continue through the month as you did the last.

GIVING THE WATER ELIXIR TO GAIA

You have created your sacred water altar, focused your intention to create a crystal homeopathic elixir to heal the waters of Gaia, worked your altar from full moon to full moon, and now have bottles of elixir labeled with your prayers for the water. It is time to do your give-away for the water. Spirit directed me to give the elixir to the waters of Gaia: her rivers, streams, oceans, springs, wells, and all running waters. This not only caused me to take the elixir to the water to pray for it, but it also caused me to get outside more and be in closer relationship with the water and nature around me. The more I went out and blessed the water, the more blessings came back to me.

You might choose to make as many trips to the water to release the elixir as you have bottles or you might take the entire supply for one release. This offering of the elixir to the waters can be as simple or elaborate as you desire. The act of going to the water and offering your water altar elixir to Gaia is a ceremony and ritual in itself. You can go alone or share it with others. Every time you go to the water and offer your prayers and elixir you are deepening your relationship with it and are being an instrument of change and healing for the water.

If you live where there are rivers, streams, or an ocean you probably already have favorite places you like to visit. Take the water with you. Bless the water. As you offer the elixir to it, notice any changes that occur around you. Once I had a fish jump out of the water as I poured. At one river I visited I saw an osprey, not just once, but I saw it every time I went to that river. Sometimes I see an amethyst color flowing into the water. I might receive inspiration or feel my own emotions release. Pay attention to what is around you. It is a time for you to be connected to the water, to Spirit, to life. Explore new places. Learn about the water sources in your area. Take the elixir to as many places as possible. You might want to keep a journal of your experiences.

If you live in a city with no access to open, running water, you can still offer your elixir to Gaia. You could give the elixir to the water in a public fountain. Birds and dogs will drink from it, children might play in it, you might even wade in it yourself. All contact with the water will be blessed by your prayers and as the water evaporates it will carry your prayers with it to be recycled into clouds, rain, or snow. Or you could choose a tree to receive the elixir. I have even offered fervent prayers for the forgotten water and sent my elixir, with full intention, down the toilet to help the cleaning of sewage water. You can use a storm drain, or a bird bath. Be creative. Remember your intention. The elixir will cause positive change to the water so just take it out there.

(See plates 6–9 for photos of the author working her sacred water altar and giving the water elixir to Gaia.)

DISMANTLING THE ALTAR

There are three reasons to dismantle your water altar. One is to clean it, another is to move it, and the last is if you no longer want to maintain the altar.

Cleaning the Altar

Every once in awhile it is good to clean the altar. You need to vacuum or scrub the floor. The altar cloth may need to be washed or replaced. The smudge shell might need to be cleaned. When you are ready to clean, set all the components of your sacred water altar aside where they will not be disturbed. You might want to clean the altar between cycles while the water is out of the bowl, or you can just set the whole altar, water and all, aside. Clean the altar and replace the cloth, smudging everything. Then place the vessel and crystals back on their altar. While you are cleaning, maintain the intention of being in sacred space. Give thanks to the water you are using for cleaning. Offer blessings and thanks as you pour dirty cleaning water down the drain.

In all the years I have kept the water altar I have never found I needed to clean the crystals in the bowl or the bowl itself. I always ask the crystals if they want to be cleaned and I always get a no, but they do enjoy a time outside once in awhile. Mine seem to especially enjoy a night out under the full moon.

Moving the Altar

If you are moving to a new home and want to keep the water altar, this is easily done. Complete the cycle as best you can. On the day you have to take it apart, set aside time to thoughtfully complete the task. Smudge. Announce to the water altar that you are temporarily taking it apart so it can be moved. Transfer the elixir from the bowl into its containers. Take the altar apart, storing the components for later use. I have moved my water altar several times with no mishap. I wrap the bowl in a large towel to protect it. The amethyst and selenite get wrapped up in smaller towels, then tucked inside the bowl. When you have moved to your new home, or transferred the altar to its new location in your existing home, set it up again as you originally did and resume the water altar work. Don't forget the containers, your dipper, or any other items you use with your sacred water altar.

If you just want or need to relocate the water altar to a different place in your home you do not have to take it apart. You can just prepare the new space then move the bowl, with the crystals and water still in it, to its new home.

Permanent Dismantling

There may come a time when you no longer want to hold this altar. That is always between you and Spirit. If you find it is too much for you energetically or if it just isn't your thing then you certainly can terminate your relationship with it.

Just like breaking up responsibly in a person-to-person relationship, give thought to the reasons you want to be out of the relationship. It is better to terminate the altar work than to feel guilty about not working it or have resentment around it.

To permanently dismantle the altar, please make one last date with Spirit. Smudge. Thank the water altar for all it has been for you. Thank the water. Acknowledge the time and effort you put into this altar and all the associated blessings of your prayers and focus on water. Remove any remaining water for a last giveaway to Gaia. You can pour the elixir onto a tree or plants if you cannot get to a river or other moving water. Remove the labels you made. It is preferable to burn them in a safe place; releasing the energy you created in them. Recycle the containers. Take apart the altar. You can wash the altar cloth and use it for something else now. The same is true for the table or other pieces. Remove the crystals from the bowl. Rinse them in clear water, thanking them for their work and service and releasing them from the agreement you made with them. When you finish rinsing them, let them dry then smudge them. If you no longer want them, you could gift them to a friend or perhaps place them out in nature where they would not be disturbed. You can use the bowl for something else now or pass it on to a friend or thrift store.

The energy you used in maintaining the water altar is now available to you to use for something else.

EXCEPTION TO THE RULE

When I received the instructions to make the water altar, I understood that the elixir created was for the healing of the waters. I was to give the elixir to Gaia. I never got that it was for personal use. I never drank it, bathed with it or otherwise used it for myself. I never offered it to others as a healing agent.

Then, a large cyst developed in my ear that would not heal. For weeks I tried everything I could think of to resolve it. Nothing worked. It hurt. I was in a lot of discomfort. Finally, in desperation, I went to the water altar and asked Spirit if I could use the elixir for myself; to heal my ear. I got a yes. Expressing my gratitude, I took a spoonful of the sacred water, soaked a cotton swab in it, and rubbed it on the cyst. It felt soothing. There was no other sensation except a sense of peace. I thanked the water and went to bed.

The next morning the cyst was gone.

Since then I have continued to only use the elixir from the sacred water altar for the waters of Gaia but it seems there is always the possibility of an exception to the rule.

You may receive guidance for the use of your water altar other than the instructions in this book. Sit with your water altar. Create a relationship with it and communicate your intention to be in service for the healing of the waters. Trust where Spirit leads you. We all share this earth but walk different paths. Water takes many different forms, from liquid to gas to solid, and flows through countless pathways across the planet and beyond. There will always be a place for you, your water altar, and your prayers for Gaia.

14

Journey

Ancient Water Spirits

☀ Intention

Our intention is to travel to meet ancient guardian water spirits and learn from them.

Breathe in. Let your ribs expand to make more room for your incoming breath. Exhale. As the air leaves your lungs push all of it out. Inhale. Expand. Exhale. Inhale. As your body expands to receive the breath, let your consciousness expand as well. Inhale. Exhale. Expand.

You are walking across a huge expanse of wide-open prairies. The ground is a rich red dirt marked with oceans of green sagebrush. A gentle wind blows warm air across your face. You can smell the sagebrush. You can smell the dirt. The sky above you is vast; a great dome of blue for as far as you can see. A few puffy clouds float lazily off over the horizon.

You walk without any food or water. It is just you out here. Walking across this big country under a bigger sky, the ground is hard under

Ancient water spirits
(Illustration by Patricia Catlett)

your feet, baked as clay under the constant sun. Notice your feet on the ground. Notice how you are feeling. Notice what you are wearing.

You continue to walk. The only landmarks are some red cliffs off in the distance. You walk in that direction. Walk toward the cliffs. You are surprised how far away the cliffs are. They seemed to be closer but you keep walking. The distance is deceiving. Very little activity is around you. A rare bird or rabbit makes a brief passage. You step over a pile of old bones, their bleached white shapes giving contrast to the red dirt. It is quiet, very quiet. All you can hear is the sound of your footsteps on the ground, the wind, your own breath, your own heartbeat.

The ground is so flat. It goes on for miles. You start to feel very thirsty and wonder if there is any water around. Water—as you think about your rising thirst you realize this prairie is as wide and vast as the ocean. Like the ocean there is no way to have a drink. You remember that this wide-open land once was an ocean, perhaps a million years ago. You are walking across the dry bottomland of an ancient ocean. What was it like then? An ocean of endless waves rolling toward a distant shore, the same vast sky above, a distant horizon giving promise of land, water to drink, a place to rest. The sun's rays beat down on you. Can you see the ancient waters that were once here?

It is getting hotter. You are almost at the red cliffs now. You hurry on seeking the shelter of their shady walls, eager to find water somewhere in their deep crevices. A hawk flies overhead, its cry ringing in your ears. You follow its flight pattern and see it land on one of the lower cliffs. You head in that direction.

You are so warm now, so thirsty. Oh, for a drink of water. Your steps are slower, it is harder to drag your feet across this dry ground. The hawk cries again as if giving you encouragement. It seems much closer now. Yes. The rocks are just there.

You step into the shadow of the red cliffs and feel the immediate coolness of the air here. It is such a relief to be out of the sun. You sit down and lean against the red rocks. They feel cool against your back. The hawk cries again and is right above you now. It seems to be calling you to follow it.

You watch the hawk. It circles over you and then gently flaps its wings, slowly flying away. You get up and walk, following the hawk. Up ahead you see a small path through the rocks, perhaps a deer trail. Somehow you know it will lead you to water. You follow the trail. Follow the hawk.

You wind through red canyons. Once a solid mountain, these walls were eroded away by ancient waters. The rocks even look rippled as if *from wave action. You stop and look at one rock face. It is embedded with millions of fossilized sea creatures, shells, fish skeletons, plants with waving tentacles, captured in these walls of stone. Once again you remember you are walking across an ancient ocean.*

The path rises, leading you up higher into these red canyons. Soon the fossils are replaced by ancient drawings; petroglyphs drawn by some forgotten people who dwelled among these rocks. They must have had their homes nearby. Perhaps there were grassy meadows where deer grazed. Yes! Look! There is a picture on the wall in front of you of an antlered animal. Behind it a hunter pursues with raised bow and arrow. Your excitement grows as you feel yourself drawn into this ancient world. You wonder what it was like to live with them.

The hawk cries again. You look up and follow it. Coming around the corner of these rocky canyons you enter into an open area, a small circle among the walls. Grass is growing and even a few small trees. The hawk lands on the branch of a tree and settles its wings to rest. You walk toward it, feeling the coolness of the grass on your feet. You can smell water. There must be a spring nearby. But where? The hawk suddenly rises up off the branch and flies to a dark shadow on the wall nearest the tree. You follow and discover it is a narrow opening into the rock wall.

The ground is very soft in front of this opening and even feels damp. Water must be close by. You cautiously approach and are startled by the array of petroglyphs on the wall above the cave opening— pictures of semihuman-looking beings, all drawn as stick figures. Tall bodies angle up from short looking legs and wide bare feet with human looking toes; long arms seem to wave out of their bodies, graceful hands reaching out, individual fingers etched into the stony canvas. Long necks arch up supporting heads of geometric shapes; triangular, square, oval, or round. Their faces have eyes drawn like spirals, mouths shaped in small circles. On top of each head, strange looking headdresses sit bearing curled horns, feathers, even rods topped with star shapes. Some hold strange forked staffs in their hands. Vessels are drawn sitting at their feet. And below them is the unmistakable image of a river running right into the wall of the red cliff in front of you . . . into a cave.

You step inside the cave. It is very dark, cool. A musty smell greets your senses. As your eyes adjust to the darkness, your senses of smell and hearing acutely focus on your surroundings. You feel the cool, damp ground under your feet. You walk further into the cave. You can smell the water nearby.

The light behind you from outside is mostly blocked by the inner walls but you can see enough to go forward. You run your hand over the cave wall and can feel more figures etched into the stone. Looking closely, you see the clear picture of a hawk. Ah, your friend guides you still! Keeping your hand on the wall you walk slowly forward. You feel the wall curve off to your right. The smell of water is stronger now. You can feel drops of it seeping on the rock wall. Moistening your fingers with these drops you place your fingers into your mouth, letting the water wet your tongue.

Rounding the corner you enter into a small room. A narrow shaft of light shines down through an opening above you. Grass grows in a thick carpet but still you do not see the water. Suddenly some movement catches your attention from the corner of your eye. You look. Nothing. There, again! Something is moving in here. You become very still and quietly wait; watching. Yes. There against the wall, three figures are quietly moving toward you. They look exactly like the stone people you saw drawn into the wall outside the cave! But these beings are alive! They are moving gracefully, silently, toward you. And their faces! Their beautiful faces! Their eyes are like stars; like galaxies *slowly turning in their eyes, looking at you, taking you in. You feel an incredible sense of awe, of peace. Their round mouths smile at you. As they come closer you can see your friend Hawk rides on the shoulders of the first one. The second one carries a beautiful stone jug. The third one holds a forked rod with a glowing star on the top.*

They are the guardians of the water; ancient water spirits who have dwelled here since the earth began. And they have come to see you; to let themselves be known to you. Reach out with your heart and listen. You can hear them in your heart. They are greeting you. Listen. What do they say to you?

They are standing around you now. You can feel their gentle power, the power of ancient wisdom and knowledge. They feel the thirst inside you, the thirst for water, and the thirst for knowledge. The being with the rod gently strikes it on the rock wall. Water pours forth from the rock. You reach out your hands to cup the precious liquid and bring it to your mouth to drink. What does this pure, beautiful water taste like? How does it feel moving in your mouth? Down your throat? Into your cells? Drink this water.

The being with the vessel holds it under the streaming water, filling the vessel, allowing the water to overflow and spill out to form a pool of crystal clear water. You drop to the ground, drinking from the pool. The hawk flies over, lands on the ground next to you, and sets its beak into the pool to drink. Then Hawk gently touches you. Feel its touch. Now Hawk directs you to look into the water. As you gaze into it you see your reflection with these ancient ones standing around you.

The water gently ripples and the scene changes. You are looking back in time, to a time when these beings freely walked the earth on this very land. Look. What do you see? Who are these beings? Where did they come from? What secrets do they share with you?

What is this place Hawk has brought you to today? See the story of these ancient ones reflected in the water. Drink it in. What happened to them? Where did they go? Why did they leave?

Now the rod being dips his star-topped rod into the water. Ripples scatter the images. You are back in the cave with the water guardian spirits, with Hawk. As they have shared their secrets with you, they also each have a gift for you. The guardian carrying the forked rod holds it out to you, offering it to you. You understand it is a divining rod, a rod to lead you to divine your truth so the waters of Spirit will always flow within you. The star on top of it glows, promising you will always have guidance. You take the rod and thank the rod being for its gift. How does this divining rod feel as you hold it? How will you use it?

The guardian with the vessel holds the vessel out and hands that to you now. This vessel is a grail to hold your spiritual wealth so that you may always drink from it and never be thirsty. What does this grail look like? Notice the details of it. Look inside it. What do you see inside the grail? You accept the grail and thank the vessel being.

The hawk guardian lifts his hand and Hawk hops onto it. The guardian whispers to Hawk and extends his hand out toward you. Hawk flaps its wings and shrinks down in size becoming a beautiful pendant. The hawk guardian slips the pendant around your neck making Hawk your personal guide and guardian. How does it feel to have Hawk with you? How do you communicate with Hawk? Does Hawk have a secret name it shares with you? Feel the power of Hawk with you. Thank the hawk guardian for this precious gift.

Filled with incredible gratitude, you discover you have gifts for these ancient beings. What is it you give to them? Offer your gifts to them now. They are pleased to accept your gifts. Take this time to listen to any further wisdom they may have for you. Listen. You may ask any question you might have for them. Ask. Listen for their reply.

Now they step back and away from you and retreat toward the red wall. They step back into the wall and, once again, become petro-glyphs. For a brief moment you see the gleam in Hawk's eye, the flash of the star on top of the rod, the sparkle of water from a stone vessel.

After a time you turn back to the pool, take one more long drink of this pure water. Feeling sated and refreshed, you begin to retrace your steps out of the cave, carrying your grail vessel and divining rod. The hawk pendant around your neck feels warm against your skin and presses into you, as if it is indeed guiding you back through the darker passage and out of the cave.

You emerge from the cave and look behind you to see the narrow opening close. Only solid rock is visible now. With three star-eyed beings smiling back at you, you raise your hand in a farewell gesture, turn, and walk away.

Return now to this time and space. Breathing in. Breathing out. And you are back.

15

Our Water on Drugs

IT ISN'T JUST INDUSTRIAL POLLUTERS who are fouling our water. You and I do it, too. Think of what we dump down the drain every day: shampoo, toothpaste, body waste filled with remains of whatever chemical preservatives were in our food, household cleaners, chemicals, engine oil, factory sludge, garbage, phosphates from our clothing and dish detergents, bath soap, dyes, perfumes. It all goes back into the water system.

EFFECTS OF MODERN SOCIETY ON THE WATER

Caffeine levels in Seattle and other major cities have been used to detect the levels of human waste that flow from sewer systems into the surrounding water. Because only people consume caffeine, and because it "remains virtually unchanged as it passes through the body," this method in the past made it easy to track the general flow of waste that escaped from cracked sewer pipes.[1] It turns out that Seattleites, enduring many cold and cloudy days, have taken too much refuge in coffee shops. Over a year of testing the water in the Puget Sound, the harbor whose water laps up against Seattle, Scott Mickelson, chief microbiologist for King County water quality control, discovered that "caffeine was found in more than

160 of 216 samples and at depths of up to 640 feet." Mickelson says, "We were very surprised to find caffeine everywhere." The article also reported that one automatic sampler in the Duwamish River, which flows into Seattle and empties into Puget Sound's Elliot Bay, measured sewage overflow between 4 and 8 a.m. and another between 4 and 8:30 a.m. "Despite the small difference, the second sampler showed total caffeine levels eight times higher than the first."[2]

I can easily imagine the scenario: people on their way to work gulping down the last of their coffee before they leave the house or stopping by a drive-through to get their 16- or 20-ounce latte for the commute. Arriving at work around 8 a.m., they soon find themselves in the queue for the restrooms down the hall. Across the city thousands of flushes cause the local sewer system to max out and push the overload through any cracks in the pipes and into the waters of Puget Sound. The unwitting synchronization of kidneys is not the only cause of the caffeine overload. Street vendors selling espresso from carts are known to dump coffee remains into storm sewers as do people who simply toss the remains of their coffee out the car window or into the sidewalk gutter where the copious rains wash the remains directly into the Sound.

The research clearly shows our human influence on the water, all the life within it, and all the life that uses it; such as fish and clams, trees, birds, or even a dog that happily swims and laps up a drink as it plays. And it isn't just wild salmon being poached in coffee that we need to think about.

Gary G. Kohls, M.D., reports on alarming results from research by environmental toxicologists who, for over a decade, "have been doing chemical analyses on the water of lakes, streams and aquifers that are the sources of public drinking water, especially the waters that are downstream from wastewater treatment facilities." According to Dr. Kohls, "The tests have consistently found measurable levels of prescription drugs, including arthritis drugs, contraceptives, psychostimulants, tranquilizers and antidepressants like Prozac, as well as cosmetics and synthetic food additives like dyes and preservatives that are excreted down the drain through the pill-popping public's kidneys."[3]

Kohls states, "Frogs in Minnesota were being turned into sterile hermaphrodites by the estrogen mimic, Atrazine, which is ubiquitous in the runoff water from the farming industry." Atrazine is banned in Europe but is one of the most widely used herbicides in the United States. It is associated with birth defects and menstrual problems when consumed by humans and is widespread in the drinking water supply in farming regions. As described by Kohls, research has revealed that alligators "are developing micropenises . . . from the estrogen-mimicking pollutants in the water of the Everglades" in Florida, while "Beluga whales in the Arctic Ocean have measurable levels of ScotchGard in their blood streams, and most Americans have measurable levels of Teflon and other such fluoridated compounds in their blood."[4]

Huh? I'm not eating Teflon! Are you?

Dr. Kohls's article went on to explain that many drugs and chemicals can cross the placental barrier into the fetus, ending up in the unborn body. "Umbilical cord blood contains hundreds of toxic chemicals, many of which are known to be carcinogens." Kohls also reminds us that the vaccinations we are given are loaded with highly toxic metals such as aluminum and mercury. Dr. Kohls reported that these chemicals enter the public water supply "through human urination and defecation" or "flushing unused pills down the toilet or tossing them into landfills that are upstream from aquifers or streams." In fact, "environmental toxicologists from Texas have found high levels of Prozac in the brains, livers and muscle tissue of bluegills, channel catfish, and black crappies from a stream in a Dallas suburb that receives effluent from the city's wastewater treatment plant."[5]

Yes, there are drugs in our water. Water, the universal solvent, carries them into every cell of every living being on the planet—human, animal, plant, and mineral.

EXAMINE YOUR CONSUMPTION

The frightening proof of what we, as humans, are doing to the water is all around us. Take the challenge to examine how you, as a consumer, personally impact the water.

Read the labels of all soaps you use. If they contain phosphates, do not use them anymore. Phosphates contribute to the overgrowth of algae in the water and cause lakes to literally smother. Many companies stopped using phosphates due to public demand but they are still found in some brands and also in automatic dish-washing detergents. Check the label.

What about your garbage? It may end up on a barge in the ocean, or worse, just dumped into the ocean. Think of the animals living there. Balloons and plastic holding strips from six-pack beverages or even multiple packaged items, such as those you buy at wholesale food clubs, all look like potential food to ducks, fish, and other water creatures. When they swallow the plastic they can choke to death. If your garbage goes directly to a landfill, it eventually gets into the local water supply through rain runoff, or leaching into groundwater.

Try to reduce the chemicals in the products you use from toothpaste to cleaning supplies. Over the past few decades many products have been developed that promote a greener, healthier environment. Besides, less chemicals in your body is essential to healthier living.

Be conscious of the water you use. Most of us live in cities and are dependent on municipalities to provide all our water. Use filters to clean out the chlorine and toxins left in the water. Recapture all possible water. Use rain barrels outside under your gutters or roof eaves and recycle the collected water on your outside ornamental plants. (Do not drink it.) Some cities will offer a rebate on your water bill for your purchase of a rain barrel or a front-load washing machine, which uses less water than a top-fill model. I got a $25 credit for each of these items I use in my home.

Since I do not enjoy stepping into a cold shower or washing my face and hands in cold water, I keep a bucket in my shower to collect the water as it runs and turns hot. I also keep a smaller container at the bathroom sink for the same purpose, dumping that cold water into the bigger shower bucket. I collect gallons of water this way that otherwise would just go down the drain. As this water is clean, I reuse it on my numerous houseplants and rarely have to draw water from the faucet to take care of them. Another alternative is to install an on-demand water heater in the bathroom so the water is immediately hot.

I keep a container in my kitchen to collect the large amounts of gray water generated there from rinsing dishes or food preparation. This gray water is usually not completely fresh so I pour it on my outside plants and trees, or even use it to flush the toilet. Notice ways you can catch gray water. Did your dinner guests not drink all their water, tea, or coffee? Don't dump it down the sink. Put it into your collection bucket. Perhaps you like hard-boiled eggs. You have to pour off the hot water and douse the eggs in several washings of cold water. You can capture all of that water as gray water rather than pour it down the drain. Coffee drinker? I am and use a French press for my daily cuppa. Rather than pour the grounds down the garbage disposal for the sewage system to reprocess, I use the gray water to rinse the grounds out onto my plants. My beautiful datura plant especially loves it. Try to avoid using the garbage disposal for anything other than the dregs left from cleaning up. Dump garbage into a compost pile or into your outside bin for pick up. All material that goes down the disposal requires water to purify it.

Whether you live in Seattle or the desert, conserving water is essential. Each effort you make is vital. There are so many obvious things to remember, things we have heard for decades. Don't let the water run while brushing your teeth, rinsing dishes, or engaging in other mindless tasks that waste water. Take shorter showers. When bathing, don't keep draining and refilling with more hot water. It is a luxury to have a long hot bath. Save it for special times when you really need it. Do the laundry or run the dishwasher only when you have a full load. Washing your car? Find out if the local car wash recycles the water. If you wash it at home, do not let the hose run. Do you really need to wash the car?

Have an awareness of the water. Say thank you to it when you shower, drink it, and do the dishes. Keep your labels of love on your water bottles. Write positive words on the pipes. Find other ways to recycle water and reduce your usage.

Get involved with local water restoration projects.

Keep the waters of your body healthy. Hydrate by drinking purified water and eat foods with water in them, such as jicama, juicy bell peppers, or watermelon. Avoid drinks with chemicals and preservatives. The more personal our water awareness is to us the more we are inclined to take care of it. Remember, you are about 70 percent water.

Many books have been written sharing the expertise of water ecology. It is not the purpose of this book to try to recap all that knowledge or repeat messages. I encourage you to read, learn, and discover ways to optimize your water awareness and usage. Technology has given us devices to reduce the flow in showerheads, toilets, and washing machines. More attention is being directed at this critical area of our lives. Please utilize all the opportunities available to you to be a more responsible water consumer.

The water, and plants, and all the earth, give to us so we might live. We truly owe them our thanks and blessings. We have been raised in a culture of consumerism—of use and throw away and buy new—of wastefulness. I am not suggesting we go into a scarcity mindset. We live in an abundant and generous universe. We are in an intricately connected relationship with that universe and all its components. All life depends on it. Being more mindful of how we interact with water helps us to expand that awareness into other areas of our lives that might also be in need of evaluation and change.

Even if you live in a place where water is abundant and free flowing, it is still a good practice to conserve. The balance on Earth is definitely in flux. Floods, droughts, and pollution all remind us of our dependency on the natural, basic, elemental gifts of Gaia. Using the sacred water altar is a specific way to interact with water, to learn from it, and to help transform it to a more purified condition. When we give back, returning the blessings we are so freely given, we keep the sacred flow moving.

16

Journey

Healing the Waters of Gaia

☀ Intention

To journey to find the source of pollution in water and to transform it by using your sacred water altar and prayers.

If you already have a sacred water altar, sit with it now and be ready to access it. If you will be taking this journey with friends, you may all share one altar or have your own individual ones. If you don't already have a water altar, you can make a simple one for this journey with a bowl of water and a crystal to stir it with.

This journey will be in two parts. At the end of Part 1, you will come back from the journey, physically access and activate your water altar, then return into the journey for Part 2. Stay in journey mode by not speaking to anyone except for when you are instructed to offer prayers.

PART 1

Breathe in. Breathe out. Let your breaths be as gentle waves moving across the ocean. In. Out. In. Out. Relax. See or feel yourself to be by the ocean. Smell the salty air; hear the sound of the waves. Perhaps you hear seagulls crying or feel the warm sand under your feet. Know the Spirit of water is around you.

Our guide for this journey is coming for you, coming to take you to a wonderful place. Our guide is a beautiful white eagle. White Eagle flies into your awareness and asks if you want to go with her. Feeling a great sense of trust with her, you agree. You find yourself sitting on her back, or perhaps being gently carried in her talons or beak. Her great wings lift and carry you out over the water and then higher into the sky. Strong muscles propel you on this journey. You feel safe, thrilled to be flying with this magnificent being. How does it feel? What do you see? What do you smell? Enjoy your experience with White Eagle.

White Eagle brings you to a beautiful primeval forest, setting you down on the soft, fragrant ground at the edge of it. You are dressed in ceremonial clothing. Perhaps you see yourself as a priestess or a priest. Long, flowing robes adorn your body. What do they look like? Something is on your head. Is it a crown? What about your feet? Are you barefooted? Do you wear sandals or shoes? Notice how you look.

See yourself at the edge of this great forest. Smell the air. It is full of the scent of pine and cedar. You can smell the rich, loamy carpet of the forest floor. It is damp from recent rain. Feel the presence of the trees. Breathe in the forest air. Feel the ground beneath your feet. Smell the smells. Listen to the sounds of the great forest. Walk among the trees. Enjoy the forest.

You come to a beautiful, huge old tree. It is the biggest tree you have ever seen. Ancient, its roots spread out in a wide circle from its thick trunk. You are drawn to come close to this great tree. Walk around it. Be with the tree. You notice that there is a doorway at the base of its trunk. The doorway is shaped like a crescent moon and is silvery, shimmery, sparkly. It seems to be more liquid than solid. Notice all you can about the door. You see there is a handle in this crescent-shaped door. Notice the handle on the door. Take hold of it. Lift it up. Pull it out. The door opens. Looking through the doorway you see stairs going down inside the tree.

Go through the doorway and step onto these stairs. You are safe and welcome here. The stairs are carved from stone—wide, cool, and smooth. There are torches lit and placed along the walls in beautiful sconces. Torches of crystal light, their beautiful colors shine and sparkle, making the walls glow with reflective light.

You begin your descent down the stairs, going down, and down. You feel the coolness of the air. It is moist with a fine mist. You can hear the sound of water below you.

The sound of water is louder now. You come to a circular platform with a railing around it. You stand on the platform. The sound of water is even louder now. Looking down, over the platform edge, you can see the water below you. What you are seeing is the primal source of water. What does it look like? How does it move? What does it smell like? How are you feeling? You lie down on this platform and reach your hand out to the water below you. Your long robes flow out around you as you reach out to the water.

As you reach out to the water it becomes very still; a reflective pool. You can see yourself reflected in it. See how beautiful you are. As you look into the water you realize that you are a part of this source of all life; part of the water.

A ripple moves across the surface of the pool. As you watch, a beautiful woman rises up out of the pool. Her body is made of water—

flowing, moving, breathing in and out like the tides. It is Gaia. There is a blissful feeling of love coming from Gaia. Feel her love for you. Her arms are like rivers, or waves. They reach out to you now. Feel her arms come around you. You are safe in her arms. Holding you, Gaia gently carries you down into the pool with her; into the water. As she does, she gently inserts something into you so you can breathe in the water.

Now you are breathing in the water with Gaia. She takes you down into it, deeper and deeper. As you go deeper into the water, you come to see, feel, hear, or know things about the water. Reach out. Connect with the water. Notice how you feel in it; how you move in it. Explore it. Experience it. Receive any information the water or Gaia has for you. Water is essential to life. You come to know the reflection of this in your own body. As the water flows and moves it gives life, as your blood gives you life. Can you talk to the water? Can you talk to your blood?

Gaia now brings you to a room in the water. This room is transparent and seems to be made of water itself. You see a porthole window in one wall. What is the window shaped like? Is it big or small? You go to the window and look through it. On the other side of that window the water is dramatically different. It is murky, polluted, dirty, in chaos. This polluted water is crying out, asking you for help. What does this polluted water look like? How do feel looking at it? What do you see or feel or know to be happening to it? How did it get to be in this polluted condition? Who can you see in this polluted water? What is the water asking of you? What are the beings you see in the water asking of you? What is needed for the water and the beings in it to be restored? Is there anything you know that you can do to help? Hold this vision and this information. Hold it so you may remember it and return to it.

COMING BACK TO
WORK THE WATER ALTAR

Hold the images and messages you have received. Shift your awareness gradually back to the current time and place. As you come back, you see your water altar sitting in front of you. Based on what you have just seen or learned in the journey, or from what you are feeling in your heart at this moment, stir the water in your altar. Speak the prayers inspired in you as you gazed upon the polluted waters. As you speak your prayers, let your words and intentions go into the water. Let them diffuse into all the molecules of the water. Hold your hands over the water and send your love into it. Let your love pour out of your hands and into the water. Thank the water. Tell it that you love it. Visualize the water clean, free of pollution, flowing freely to all beings, restored. Stir the waters of the altar with your crystal wand. Speak your words. Visualize the change you desire for the water. Stir the water. Send the water your love.

When you feel complete with your prayers at the water altar, return to a comfortable position and resume your deep, relaxing breaths as before, preparing to return to your journey.

PART 2

Breathe and relax. Return to the ocean, breathing. Breathe in like the tide moving toward shore. Breathe out like the waters returning to the ocean. Reconnect with your images or feelings of being in the pool with Gaia. Go back to the room where the transparent wall and porthole window were separating the source water from the polluted water. Allow yourself to be back there, back in that place. Look through the porthole window again. Observe the water.

See how the water has changed since you offered your prayers for the healing of the waters at your sacred water altar. See how your prayers changed the situation. How have the polluted water and the beings in the water changed?

Receive any new information being offered to you. What informa-tion is being given or shown to you? Perhaps there is a special guide who wants to come and work your altar with you. Talk with your guide. Make a connection, a bond, with this guide. Ask this guide any questions you may have.

Take some time to just be with the water. Talk to the water. Sing to the water. Ask how you can help the waters of Gaia to heal. How can you help the waters of your own body heal? What is the water of-fering to you? How is it offering to help you? See yourself as a priestess or priest of the waters.

It is time now to leave this place. Offer your thanks to the water, to Gaia, and to any other guides who helped you. Now Gaia holds you and carries you gently back up through the water to the source pool. Back onto the platform. Turn to look back behind you at the source water. Feel its gratitude. Feel the love of the water, of Gaia. As you stand on the platform, a gift is offered to you. What is the gift? How will you use it? Accept this gift now. You find that you have a gift to of-fer in return. Offer your gift now to the water, to Gaia, to your guide. What is it you gift to them?

It is time to go now. You turn around, walking off the platform, back to the stairs. Walk up the stairs, out the crescent-moon door of the tree, and back into the forest.

Look up at the trees. See the moon and stars shining above you. Breathe with the trees. Feel the flow of water and life in your body and all of life. Feel that connection. Know you can return to this place anytime you want to. You are always welcome here.

Feel your breath again within you; breathing in, out, back in this time and place, in your body, the water living within you. Breathe. Ground and center yourself back into the present.

17

Water for Gaia

ON THE FULL MOON NIGHT of March 2000 an exceptional minus 3-foot tide was predicted, giving me a rare opportunity to make offerings of the water altar at the edge of Seattle's Puget Sound.

As we all know, the moon controls the tides but charting the tides is a precise marine science. The high and low tide information for each day is vital to people who interact with the oceanic waters. Boaters, fishermen, ferryboat captains, and people who trek out to the beaches to dig for clams all rely on tide tables. The local newspapers include the information in the weather section.

During these rare minus tide hours, the moon, flexing her cosmic muscles, pulls the water far out and away from its usual retreat line from the shore. It is a magical time to walk the beach. Tide pools, filled with exotic-looking sea creatures, allow close-up examination of life-forms that normally are hidden underwater. The sand of the beach blends into a field of rocks, large and small, slippery with seaweed, and encrusted with barnacles. These silent sentinels sit squashed into a deep layer of ancient stones worn to pebbles by the constant washing of the waves.

My home was close to Golden Gardens Beach, a waterfront area with a sandy strip stretching for miles along the salty, tide-influenced waters coming in through the Straits of Juan de Fuca from the Pacific

Ocean. A large marina housed hundreds of boats, moored by locals, waiting to leave their slips and sail out on the cold waters, enjoying magnificent views of the Olympic Mountain range directly west across the water. Past the marina, a perfect beach lines the water for miles to the north until the terrain changes to rocks and trees. Tall fir and cedar trees border the sandy expanse to the east, creating a lush contrast with the water. Through the trees, a train track parallels this beach connecting Seattle to smaller towns to the north and south.

I had been looking forward to this night for at least a week. A minus 3-foot tide is fairly rare and about as low as tide levels drop. Finally! The time had come. After completing the water altar ceremony in my altar room, I collected my ceremonial tools: a bundle of sage, my abalone shell, a large feather for smudging, candles, an altar cloth, and of course, the bottles of elixir from the water altar. Loading it all into a backpack, along with a flashlight, I drove the short distance to Golden Gardens. Parking in the daytime was always a challenge due to the popularity of the place, but tonight only a few cars were there. Good. Not crowded. I parked and took a moment to consciously breathe, being present in the moment and in my intention to create a ceremony to offer this sacred elixir to Gaia.

The drumbeats from the beach were audible before I left the car. I got out, hoisted the backpack over one shoulder, and started walking toward the beach. Bonfire-lit circles clustered under the brilliant full moon. Shadows danced across the sand in rhythm with drummers' hands pounding out primal messages on skins of animals stretched taut across wooden frames. The cadence of voices and drums, rising and falling to an ancient tempo, was conducted by cellular memories deep within their swaying bodies. The ancient celebration of the heartbeat of the Mother was being honored and performed by her children.

The great ebb of the minus tide drew me toward the northern end of the beach, away from the drum circles. No one else had ventured down this far. The rich smells of low tide were delivered by a mere whisper of a breeze. The night was cool but not cold. I was very comfortable walking along the shore.

I felt enchanted by the magic of the moment. The moon demanded my presence and I obeyed. I walked with her, that great silver ghost crab, as she sidled across her appointed path, traversing the black beach of night. Far from its usual boundary, the water lapped lazily in small, frothy waves. Following the shining walkway, I felt the profound feminine energy of Gaia, the Mother. It was all around me in the moonlight, in the soft and gentle movement of the water. I was aware of my own female body responding to the night. My senses were heightened to all the smells, the music of the water moving across the rocky beach, my eyes growing accustomed to the natural light of night. My breath entrained with the rhythm of the water. I felt in sync with my surroundings; totally present in the moment, no thoughts or worries, just the total experience of being in this beautiful place under the full moon.

The exceptional low tide exposed the beach, like a shy lover gradually dropping her gauzy nightgown to share her secret beauty with her beloved. Moving toward the outward edge of the Sound, I kept the light from my flashlight moving ahead of me, cautious of each footstep as I intruded upon the seldom-disturbed realms of sea creatures caught out in the lunar light, vulnerable now to my approach. The moon was so bright I realized I did not need the artificial rays to seek out their hiding places. I turned off the switch and stashed the flashlight in my backpack.

The moonlight provided the pathway for me to follow, illuminating this watery world. Full of childlike wonder I followed it. Scattered through the rocks were the bright colors of starfish, anemones, sea cucumbers, and sea pens wedged under black boulders still dripping from being recently underwater. Some of these shy creatures had migrated out into the moonlit expanse of beach, scattering themselves among abandoned shells of clams, and the armless remnants of red crabs. A piece of seaweed, spread out across a sandy section of the beach, looked like a fan dropped, perhaps, by some exotic sea dancer as she retreated to privacy behind watery curtains.

Lost in the peaceful quiet of the night, the loud metallic sound of a train, speeding down the track behind me, jarred me into a momentary reminder of the closeness of the city. As the train moved southward along the tracks, the moon filled in the tunnel of its passing with her etheric glow. Silence returned.

I moved away from the water's edge and sat on a dry rock under a cedar tree, its shadows lacing the sand at my feet. Setting the backpack down, I looked up at the stars. Immersed in the moment I felt a part of all that was above me, below me, before me, behind me, within me. The vast, night sky reminded me of being told in school that the starlight we see from Earth left its source long ago. Tonight the moon was so bright I could not see any stars. I wondered, are they still out there? Those stellar beings? Or could it be that those stars, upstaged by the great luminous orb of the moon, were now the colorful inhabitants I saw hiding under the rocks, clinging by tenacious arms to the sea stones? Were they here now, part of some cosmic exodus, leaving their astral addresses for the diminutive domains of these seascape dwellings? Had the stars come here to live and be blessed by the moonlit waters of the Earth Mother? To be rocked in the salty cradle of her tides? Did they share secret myths of star voyages through the whispering of seashells held to an inquiring ear?

I felt a great and ancient secret was being revealed to me. Raising my arms upward to the night, the words seemed to flow out of me:

> *O, Star Nations of the Sea! You sunflower stars, you sea bats, you orange baskets, blue brittles, and red stars! You dwarf novas of forgotten lineages living in the rocky constellations of the shore. Do the oysters and clams and forests of kelp know the truth about you? Are you the seeds of the heavenly bodies that shine above? Star seeds planted by feathered gods, encoded with mystic navigational messages? If I hold your pinwheeled arms in mine, will we rise up on*

*the mist above the water, past the moon, and shine
in constellations viewed by nocturnal beach walkers
of another world?*

Moonlight shimmered over me and the beach began to fade away below me, as I began to rise upward. I found myself riding through the night, propelled by slowly spinning starfish swimming through galactic channels toward their ancestral home. Tonight I was part of that ancient cosmic voyage, making my own passage between the worlds. Looking down I could see luminous rays of moonlight spreading out over the waters. What could I bring from my earthly life to offer in these starry realms?

Deep within me I heard the stars and moon answer with an invocation of their own: "Rise up, Priestess of the Waters. Take on the vestments of your altar. Carry the message we have instilled in you. Serve the waters. Serve the Earth and all her children."

The stars surrounded me in a silent embrace. I hung in the sky with them, part of them, turning on galactic arms as pinwheeled as those of the starfish from the beach; slowly spinning, shining. But tonight belonged to the moon. Gradually I could feel the pull of her within my body; pulling me down, my body getting heavier.

The coldness of the rock I sat upon seeped through my clothes. My breath moved within me. I was on the beach again.

I stood up, hoisted my backpack, and walked out toward the water. It was time to fully embrace this calling. Yes. I am a priestess—for Gaia—for the water.

A low, flat rock caught my attention. It looked like an altar just waiting for a wandering water priestess to make her ceremonial offerings. I accepted its silent invitation and stood behind it. Opening the backpack I removed my tools. The deep purple of the altar cloth splashed its color onto the sand as it draped over the stone. Striking a match, I lit one tea candle and placed it in the center of the cloth. Taking the six bottles of the elixir, filled earlier tonight from the water altar, I positioned them in a circle around the candle. Abalone shell, sage, and feather followed. I ignited the sage in the candle flame, let it catch fire, then blew out the flame, resting the smoldering and pungent stick in the shell. Using my feather, I moved the smoke over and around my body, the altar, and bottles holding the elixir.

Raising my arms up to the moon, the great queen of the night, I faced the west calling to the Spirits of that direction, thanking them for opening this portal tonight into the realm of the water, the sea creatures, and for my voyage through their gateway into the stars. "Thank you, beloved ones of the west. Thank you for hearing my prayers."

Listening to the waves' lilting music I added my own voice, singing in harmony with the water and the night. No words were in my song. I was chanting with ancient voices I could hear all around me, in praise of the water, the moon, and all the creatures of the earth, and to Gaia, our Mother. Picking up two of the bottles of water, I walked the distance to the edge of the Sound, again marveling at the far distance the water was from shore.

Holding the water up as an offering, I spoke my prayers for the water, for Gaia. I sent my prayers out over the gentle waves, watching my words ride across the crests of foam like little boats. Kneeling down onto the soft sand and pebbles between the bigger rocks, I poured the contents out of the bottles, visualizing all the waters of Puget Sound filling with the purple glow of the amethyst-infused elixir, watching it swirl away on a moonlit current.

Walking back to the altar rock, I took two more bottles, returned to the far edge of the water and repeated my prayers, again offering the elixir to Gaia.

"Thank you, Water, for your gift of life. I see you clean and restored."

Walking back to the altar rock for the last two bottles, I heard a very loud, roaring sound. It had been so silent and I had seen no one else arrive; what could this sound be? Maybe it was another train? It was surely loud enough to be one. But no, that couldn't be. My back to the water, I was facing the train tracks and no train was in sight. The roaring was coming from behind me. Perhaps a boat was going by in the night? Or maybe it was one of the local seaplanes out for a moonlit joyride?

I turned and looked. There was no boat, no plane. Just me and the water that had rushed up to meet me at the rock! The tide was still very far out away from shore. The exposed beach still spread out on either side of me. But here, just here at the altar, the water had come to me! I felt it had come to thank me for my offerings. I fell to my knees to embrace this moment, the salt of my tears joining the salt of the Sound. As the water retreated back to the far edge of the beach, I poured the last two bottles of the elixir onto the wet sand and watched it journey back to the sea, trailing its amethyst light behind it.

I sat with the water, the sea creatures, and the moon for a long time. Finally, I gathered my ceremonial things, offered a last prayer in gratitude for this magical night, and started to walk back.

I have no idea of how much time had elapsed. It seemed like hours—lifetimes. The moon had risen high into the sky and the air felt colder. I walked slowly south along the edge of the water, not wanting this night to end. Loud splashing sounds broke the silence as two seals frolicked in the moonlight.

I heard the distant beat of a lone drummer and smelled the smoky remnants of smoldering logs. The light of dying bonfires reflected across the night and hung above the water. Small shells crunched under my feet. Reveling in this symphony, I took one last look back down the beach, and slowly walked away.

18

Journey

Moon Woman

✺ Intention

We journey to the moon for a cleansing of the emotional body.

Focus on your breath. Inhale. Then breathe out, allowing your breath to anchor your body. Breathe in again, inviting your consciousness and awareness to lift up. Exhale. Inhale, lifting up with your breath, your breath lifting you up and away.

You are walking along the edge of the water on a lovely evening. The sun has just set. The light is dimming. Perhaps you are by a river, a lake, or the ocean. The water is calm and inviting looking. The air smells fresh and clean. It is quiet and you are alone. You find a comfortable place to sit down and look out across the water. As it gets darker you settle into your spot, content to watch the change from day to night. The moon has not yet risen and stars have not yet emerged from the darkening sky. Notice your surroundings, how you are feeling.

Notice any sounds or smells around you in this soothing place.

Across the water you notice a glow of light just at the horizon. You shift your focus to watch as it grows from a glow into a rounded arc of light. The light lifts up from below the horizon and begins to rise in the sky. The light is luminous and golden; soft and beautiful. You feel a thrill within you as you realize the light is from the full moon rising directly across the water in front of you. Steadily it reveals itself as it rises in the sky. You wonder what ancient power has set this incredible event into motion. What holds the moon in the sky? The moon continues to reveal the roundness of her body until a full, glowing orb is hovering right above the water, in front of you. The sky seems to reach out and enfold her; to cradle her in gentle, invisible arms as she shines.

The light from the moon continues to expand out into the darkness. It shines on the water in front of you, spreading out across the surface, and comes right up to the shore. You get up from your spot and walk to the edge where the land meets the moonlit water. You step into the water, feeling the cool liquid flowing across your feet. You look down at your feet and see that the light shining on them makes them glow. Your feet feel a wonderful tingling, an aliveness, as if they have taken on an awareness of their own. You feel this glowing and tingling rise up into your belly, into your second chakra. The moonlight is filling up your second chakra, making it glow.

You take a few more steps out into the water, keeping your feet on the light. Another step; you no longer feel the cool water on your feet. Instead of the water you are standing on the light itself. The light lifts you up out of the water. As you rise up out of the water you realize you are standing on a stairway made of moonlight. The stairway rises all the way up to the moon. You begin to walk up the moonlight stairs . . . stepping up, and up. And now the stairway seems to be moving you along like an illuminated escalator. You rise up higher and higher on the light of the moon. Your second chakra is shining with the light of the moon. If anyone looked up at you from below, it would appear that another moon is rising from the water to join the queen of the night shining above you.

How does it feel to rise up into the night, pulled toward the moon on these golden stairs? Look around you and notice the night illuminated by this heavenly orb's light. What can you see in the moonlight? Your body is glowing as you rise. Can you feel your body glow? Notice how you are feeling.

Look up at the moon as you come closer to it. You can see the dark shapes of craters where meteorites have hit and pitted its surface. You feel your second chakra filled with the moon's light. Is your second chakra also filled with craters? Are you carrying scars of emotional damage within you? The moon shines through you, illuminating you. What is revealed in you?

As you come closer to the moon, look at the Earth below you, shining blue with the waters. Can you see the reflected glow of the moon on the Earth? Can you see the reflected glow of your own illuminated body shining on the Earth's surface? Perhaps your light creates a shadow on the Earth's surface.

The higher you rise, the lighter you feel—the less you feel the pull of the Earth's gravity. You are entering into the more subtle draw of the moon. It seems to tug and pull at you from your second chakra. Feel the lunar energy moving within you. Let the moon lure you in.

As you come deeper into her field you see a set of very large, ancient doors. The moving stairs of light lead right up to them. You can see beautiful carvings on the surface of the doors, perhaps runes, or glyphs. What do the doors look like? Now the great doors begin to slowly open to allow you entrance—entrance into the moon! The light moves you forward into the moon and then stops. It remains as a pathway under your feet as you stand inside the moon.

Looking around at the inner landscape of the moon, you realize it is mostly water—cascading waterfalls, flowing rivers, lakes, oceans, water everywhere. Notice all the moonwater. Take a good look around. Feel, smell, and experience the water inside the moon. The path you are on seems to wind endlessly through the moon, allowing access to its mysteries. What else can you see in the moon's inner landscape?

As you take in the beauty, the magnificence, of being inside the moon, a guide appears and greets you. She is Moon Woman and she welcomes you here. Notice what she looks like. Is she young or old? How is she dressed? Notice the light shining through her, around her. You feel enfolded by her presence. She asks if you are surprised that the moon is full of water. She explains to you that the water inside the moon absorbs the light and energy of the sun and radiates it out of its body, reflecting it. This causes the moon to shine and glow.

She comes very close to you. You can feel her breathe. Your breath entrains with hers. In. Out. In and out. You are breathing with Moon Woman and the moon. All the waters inside the moon are moving with your breath . . .with her breath. The waters move forward, and back. Just like the tides on Earth. Experience the tidal breath of Moon Woman. Now you know why the waters of Earth move as they do. They are also entrained with the moon's breath. Feel this beautiful, cosmic flow of water, of breath.

You feel yourself drawn back to Moon Woman. Her eyes are glowing with silver light. Her hair is flowing like waterfalls of light. She exudes peace, calm, serenity. Perhaps she has changed since you first noticed her. Is she older? Younger? Feel yourself with Moon Woman.

Moon Woman leads you to a pool of silvery water. She tells you it is the pool of lunar reflection and cleansing. Look into the water and see your reflection in it. Once again you see those craters in your second chakra—those pits, scars, and blockages in your emotional body. Moon Woman explains to you that, just like the surface of the moon, these craters represent experiences in your life. She tells you that the pool can cleanse you, not of the experiences—they are part of your landscape. But you can be cleansed of the pain and suffering caused by them.

Moon Woman takes your hand and leads you into the pool of lunar reflection and cleansing. Feel the water. Notice the feelings you have in your body, especially in your second chakra. Feel the loving support of Moon Woman.

Moon Woman takes your hands and looks into your eyes. You have a great sense of trust in her. She cradles you in her arms, then gently submerges you into the pool. Feel the water move through your body, through your chakras. Let any sadness or grief, anger or fear, wash out of you, perhaps as tears. This is a great cleansing, a great release and relief. Let the water wash it all away. Feel the water of the pool flowing through you, cleansing you. The water moves through every cell of your body, purifying each cell. You experience a feeling of weightlessness as the water supports you, flows through you, cleanses you.

Once again you become aware of Moon Woman in the water with you. Her arms are around you. She lifts you out of the water. You feel at peace. Moon Woman sets you down next to the pool. As you stand up again your chakras are flowing like a great fountain. Feel the purified energy of your chakras flowing through you.

Moon Woman would like you to always remember this time you have spent with her. She offers you a gift that is just for you. Accept her gift. Ask her any questions you might have. You also have a gift for Moon Woman. Offer it to her now.

Take this time to look around inside the moon, the water, the light.

Notice your feelings, the flowing of your cleared chakras. Notice if Moon Woman has changed again. She seems to grow older and younger while retaining all her beauty.

Moon Woman leads you now to the edge of a great waterfall. An endless surge of water is flowing out of the moon and out into the night sky. Each drop of water is illuminated and looks like a fountain of stars falling toward Earth. She looks at you again with her silver eyes and smiles. You know you will always see her face when you look at the moon.

Moon Woman takes your hand, then breathes her breath inside you. Feel her breath inside you. Look again at the water flowing out of the moon. You easily and calmly step into the water. You can feel it pulling you toward the waterfall, closer, until you are sliding down the great waterfall. You emerge from inside the moon, riding the water down toward Earth. It is like a great, fun waterslide. Enjoy the ride.

You cascade down the moon waterfall and pass through the atmosphere of the moon toward the Earth. You can see the water below you. Feel the Earth's gravity gently guiding you back to where you began. You gently splash into the water, back on Earth again. What a ride! You feel joyful and splash about in the water that seems to be a giant pool of moonlight.

As you frolic in the water, you see the full moon is setting now. You can see Moon Woman's face smiling at you. The round moon sinks lower, changing from silver to gold, until it is only a glowing arc and finally drops below the horizon. You swim to shore where towels and dry clothes await you.

As you stand on the land, breathe in. Breathe out. Feel the pure fountain of your chakras flowing. Feel the joy of this night with Moon Woman. Embrace yourself; craters and all.

And you return to this time and space.

Deepening Your Practice

In this journey we visit the moon and discover some of its physical qualities. The moon has long been associated with our emotional bodies. Our culture is full of stories of moonlight and romance as well as stories of moonlight and craziness, or lunacy. The dictionary defines lunacy as an intermittent form of insanity, which formerly was supposed to depend on changes of the moon. In alchemy, lunar energy is related to silver, the color we often associate with moonlight. In Roman mythology, Luna is the goddess of the moon, and so people thought to be insane were called lunatics.

The effect of the moon is most often felt in our emotional body, or in the second chakra. This chakra is the belly area, an area of great vulnerability for many people. Among the many second chakra qualities are the elements of water, feelings and emotions, sexuality, polarities, change, pleasure, and nurturing. While the sun is a life-giving and driving force, the moon is reflective and brings out our own reflective and intuitive feelings. The moon changes all the time. Each night it is in a little bit different phase from empty to full. Like the moon, we have our phases. We are full and radiant or feel waning, needing time to withdraw. We all have different moods during the day; we are changeable.

The moon does not generate its own light but gets its luminous glow from the sun. About 70 percent of the sunlight that reaches the moon is reflected and the rest is absorbed. That 70 percent is an interesting number as it is estimated that around 70 percent of the Earth's surface is water and about 70 percent of our human body is water.

The moon controls the waters of the Earth through the tides. Tides are produced by the gravitational attraction of the moon and the sun and reflect the alternating rise and fall in the level of the seas. Ocean tides are most obvious but tides occur in all bodies of water, and even in the atmosphere and the solid crust of the earth! Water is everywhere; and everywhere there is water, the moon has some control over it. Earth and moon are magnetically attracted to each other. The moon tries to pull Earth to her but Earth, with its stronger gravitational field, holds on and remains stable. However, the water of the planet—and our bodies—does not stay stable, it moves with the moon, causing the tides to occur.

Our experiences are recorded in our memories. These memories are stored in our bodies, in our cells. I believe it is the water of the cells that pulls the memories in and holds them there. It would then be no wonder that we are so affected by the moon as she moves our memories around in high and low tides of emotions. Since the second chakra is the energetic center of all these emotions, it is easy to imagine it pitted with the emotional hits we take during our lives. Emotional craters are indeed part of our personal landscape. The moon has craters, too, but her light still shines through them. They are just part of what the moon is. Learning to let our light shine through our own emotional craters is part of moving into the fullness of who we are, wounds and scars, craters and all.

Notice how when the moon rises and sets she has more color. The magnificent gold of the full harvest moon, or the mysterious red we sometimes see, is caused by the moon passing through the layers of the Earth's atmosphere, enhancing her color. As the moon rises up above the thicker layers closest to Earth, often full of pollution, to her position higher into the sky, her pure light shines forth as she sails through the night, in and out of the clouds. Our emotions, like the moon's light, are subject to interference. Our pure light is often obscured but it is always there.

Then there is the dark side of the moon, hidden from view. Like that unseen side of the moon, the dark side of our emotional body is always present, sometimes visible only as shadows. We don't know what is hidden there, who might be looking at it, or how is it perceived. It is a part of us that holds secrets. Who knows? They might be wonderful, secret parts of ourselves just waiting for the light to reveal them, waiting to be coaxed out to be bathed in the moonlight.

During the next month, chart your course as the moon moves from new into full. In this way you may come to understand more about how the moon—its phases and its tides—are reflected in yourself. Traditions teach us that the new moon is the time for setting intentions, which then have the next month, or moon cycle, to go through all the phases required to come to fruition when the cycle is complete at the full moon. During that time there will be low and high tides. The moon passes through a new astrological sign about every three days. Each one of these phases is felt in sometimes subtle or dramatic ways. The moon in Cancer might be very emotional while the moon in Capricorn might find us behaving in a very practical manner. How does the moon affect you? Do you feel different at different phases of the moon?

Decades ago, while living in Laramie, Wyoming, I discovered an aspect of myself that is wonderfully definitive of my personality. One lovely summer night I was in a fit of housecleaning and took my rugs outside to shake them clean. I looked up and saw the beautiful full moon filling the night with bright, silver light. Ah! What a lovely night. The next time I took my rugs out to shake them, the moon was full! At first I thought it a coincidence, but it kept happening. I started to notice that about three days before the full moon I really wanted, needed, to clean my house! Fortunately for others, this need transfers to my work place so I also end up cleaning the office. This has gone on for months, years, decades, even if I am not aware of the moon phase. With friends and family it is almost a joke. One night, while busily cleaning out the refrigerator and scrubbing floors, I received a phone call from my son. He was in a friendly, chatty mood and I was distracted. He finally asked me if something was wrong.

"No," I replied, "I am just busy cleaning."

There was a long silence on the line and then my son was laughing.

"Mom, is the moon full?"

And sure enough, it was.

19

Dr. Emoto

ABOUT A WEEK AFTER the transformational experience at Golden Gardens walking with the moon at low tide, it was time for the monthly planetary healing circle at Starfeather's house. I drove the distance from my home in Ballard north to Edmonds, a small city just over the border between King County and Snohomish County. I liked to take the rather circuitous route through the neighborhoods on the back roads, avoiding the interstate. Large fir and cedar trees lined the roads. Open spaces allowed glimpses of the nearby water of Puget Sound. An occasional eagle flew by, adding to the beauty of the drive. Tonight it was raining and windy. I could see the tall trees bending in the wind. For a moment I had a rather animated thought of them singing in the shower, washing away all the residue of polluting car emissions from their lush boughs. I laughed and sang along with the radio and the trees as the windshield wipers kept time.

Reaching my destination, I pulled into Starfeather's driveway and parked under a large cedar tree that seemed to be behaving as trees normally do. It was dripping from the rain but was not engaging in shower singing. Pulling my scarf tighter around my neck, I went through the gate and walked around the pathway to the back entrance. Starfeather lived in a split-level house; we used the main room of the lower floor, which faced her backyard, for our circle gatherings. The light from the room shone out through the sliding-glass doors, spreading a glow across the patio. Stepping inside out of the cold, I welcomed the warmth radiating out from a crackling log fire in her fireplace and the smiles of my friends. An altar was set up in the center of the room. Starfeather always created a beautiful altar for each gathering on which she placed candles, freshly cut flowers, a chalice of water, and crystals. People were gathering around, greeting one another, getting settled. We were a small group, mostly women, who met once a month to offer prayers for Gaia. One woman, Mary, brought her daughter, Hannah, with her to the circle. Hannah was a young teenager, maybe fourteen years old. She was a collective hope for us, a young person interested in these ways of Spirit. We loved having her as part of the circle, joining in prayers for Gaia.

We took turns leading the monthly circle, choosing a focus for the healing of our planet. We had prayed for peace, for the trees, even for clearing the energy of Hiroshima. Tonight it was my turn; I chose the water.

I had brought bottles of the elixir for everyone and told them about the water altar, how I had come to create it, and about Floyd. I shared my recent experiences with the water at Golden Gardens. They were all excited about this spiritual work I was learning and wanted to participate. Mary would soon be traveling to Japan, where she had previously lived, taking Hannah with her. They said they would take some of the elixir with them and release it there. How exciting—the water altar going to Japan!

At the end of circle that night I felt good; like I had shared something important. I trusted these people would continue their prayers for the water and that each of them would take time to walk to the water's edge to offer the elixir. The ride home was especially peaceful for me.

The next weeks were spent in my usual routine of clients and nights in the altar room, working with the water altar. It was a joyful time for me. I felt closely connected to Spirit. I was trusting, expanding, learning, growing, and actively creating new patterns in my life. I had been richly blessed with so much lately. That I was about to receive another huge revelation was not even in my mind. But, Spirit had yet another surprise in store for me.

A month came and went. Once again I was driving to Starfeather's for circle. No premonition prepared me for what was about to happen. I was the last to arrive. Mary and Hannah were back from Japan and everyone was clustered around them. When I walked in they all turned to look at me, with huge grins on their faces. Conversation stopped. We just looked at each other.

"What?" I asked. "What's up?"

Mary stepped forward holding a book. "Ravenwood, you are not going to believe this! I brought this back from Japan with me. You have to see it!"

"Well, what is it? Show me!"

She handed me the book. It was written by Dr. Masaru Emoto.[1] His name would later become a household word but that night we had never heard of him. Dr. Emoto had conducted lengthy experiments to prove that the conditions water is exposed to literally change the structure of the water. He had collected samples of water from different live water sources, such as pure glacial streams or polluted industrial rivers. He then froze the water and photographed the resulting crystals using a powerful microscope and camera. The photos were astonishing. The crystals formed from clear water were lovely geometric shapes, each unique, perfect, beautiful. They looked like pictures we have all seen of snowflakes, or exquisite diamonds cut by a great artisan. The polluted water crystals had no resemblance to these watery gems. Their shapes were deformed; their structure was broken and no longer cohesive. The book had pages and pages of examples. Tap water seemed overall to do badly, having no crystalline structure; the frozen samples were often dark masses with globular centers.

The next part Mary showed me almost made my heart stop beating. Dr. Emoto wanted to know what happens when we speak to water. Using distilled water for a base, he filled beakers with this neutral water, took samples, and photographed the water crystals, which were nondescript in shape or distinction. Then he printed out written words which he taped to each beaker. He let the beakers sit for a time before he froze and photographed the water. The new photographs showed distinct changes in the structure of the distilled water. The only change had been the words taped onto the beakers and yet the difference was profound.

The words changed the water.

The words that produced the most perfect and beautiful crystals were *thank you* and *love*, which had formed intricate, perfectly symmetrical crystals, with delicate, faceted points. On other beakers he taped words with negative meanings. One was *you fool*. That poor crystal had lost all integrity and looked broken and depleted.

I stared at the book in shock. He had put labels on the water just as I did with the sacred water elixir! And the water responded accordingly!

The most dramatic of these, to me, was the photograph of water that was labeled with the words, *you make me sick, I will kill you*. The resulting crystal had actually formed with a stick-figure type shape that appeared to be wearing a mask. One elbow was bent as if this figure was holding something in its hand, like a weapon. The water had formed in a very specific pattern to reflect the words.

The amazing book included pictures of water from an urban lake that was known to be polluted. The crystals seemed to be struggling to hold their shape. It looked like they were falling apart. Dr. Emoto gathered people to circle around the lake and offer prayers of thanks and love to the water. After their prayer ceremony, he took new samples from the lake, froze, and photographed them. The change was incredible. Water, whose crystals had been visibly compromised, had transformed into beautiful and balanced structures.

We pored over the book, seeing this dedicated man's work prove that water is changed by what happens to it. One chapter showed how Dr. Emoto played Mozart for some beakers of water and heavy metal music for others. Guess which beaker of water had the perfect crystals?

After playing Chopin's "Farewell Song" to one sample, his photograph revealed a most intriguing result. The basic crystal shape had divided into many equal, smaller crystals, each looking like an exact duplicate of the other but separated from each other. It was as if they were bidding farewell to one another.

In 1995, an earthquake rocked Kobe, Japan. Dr. Emoto took samples from the local tap water three days after the quake hit. The crystals were completely broken down. There was no cohesion to them; only a chaotic image of dark, blotchy shapes. Dr. Emoto wrote, "It is as if the water captured the fear, panic and deep sorrow of the people immediately after the earthquake."[2] Three months later, after "helping hands and sympathy from all over the world were given to the people of Kobe . . . people were able to restore their environment due to the kindness and warmth of others." New samples were taken of the same tap water and this time the water had formed into perfect, six-sided, filigreed crystals. Dr. Emoto commented that, "This crystal seems to have collected these feelings also."[3]

Dr. Emoto concluded that the water remembered being clean, pure, and at peace and that when it was disrupted it was trying to regain perfection. I thought of homeopathic remedies being stirred into water that remembered their qualities. I remembered moonlit water rushing up to meet me at Golden Gardens. I recalled my prayers and blessings offered when I had simply walked to the water's edge, said "Thank you, Water. Bless you, Water," and told it that I loved it. I thought of the amethyst and selenite crystals in the sacred water altar and how I came to know the elixir would remember their frequencies and share them with the water it flowed into when released from the purple-labeled bottles; bottles labeled with words of love and gratitude sending their message into the water.

I started to cry. My circle sisters held me.

"Ravenwood," Mary said, "This book is the validation of your water altar."

Yes. Here was proof. I wondered what water crystals gathered from a North Carolina river on a beautiful summer day, sunlight sparkling on the surface, a happy trout jumping out to grab a passing mayfly, would look like as compared to post-Floyd when that same water was filled with dead carcasses and millions of gallons of animal waste.

Each page in Dr. Emoto's book was a revelation. I want to honor this man, the work he has done, and his courage in taking on such a project and sharing it with the world. Several years after that night at Starfeather's, I had the opportunity to hear him speak in Sedona, Arizona. By then his work was a sensation, especially among the New Agers. The venue where he spoke was standing room only. He did not speak English but his translator told his story. At one point, she said, he had all but given up. He became too discouraged, it was too much to do. The waters were so polluted and so few people cared. But then he would spend time with his grandchildren and it was for them, the next generation, that he continued to do his work, to write, to teach. He was not a young man. Life on the road, traveling all around the world, must have been very hard on him. Yet, he did it—for the water, for the children, for Gaia.

20

Egyptian Mysteries

IN JULY OF 1999, Charla was in California visiting her family. I flew into San Francisco for a long weekend so we could have a little vacation together. One of her longtime friends, Nicki Scully, was also in town to teach a class. Charla told me Nicki was a shaman, having studied with well-known Native American elders. Nicki also had a deep passion for Egypt. She had been leading tours there for over twenty years. She also taught classes on the ancient Egyptian Mysteries, exploring the arcane spirituality of Egypt from three thousand to five thousand years ago. Charla and I went to see Nicki where she was staying at friend's home. She greeted us at the door with big hugs. She was wearing a black velvet hat with sparkles on it, and was adorned with more velvet layered in long, flowing pants, a soft sweater, and a jacket. She wore beautiful jewelry and had an infectious smile. We had a short but delightful visit with her before she had to leave. I was fascinated with her stories of her recent trip to Egypt. After we left, I kept thinking about Egyptian Mysteries and found myself remembering an incident from my senior year of high school, way back in 1967.

It was just weeks away from graduation. My two best friends, Kay and Zelma, were talking about how they wished they could go on a senior trip when school was over. I didn't know teenagers took trips by themselves. Why didn't my family talk about such things? It was nothing I had ever given any thought to. As we walked into our English class to take our seats, Kay put her books down on her desk and announced, "For my trip, I would go to Paris."

"Not me," Zelma said, sitting down in her chair, "I want to go to Rome."

Suddenly, words just popped out of my mouth. "I want to go to Cairo!" I exclaimed. I could not have been more surprised at myself.

"Cairo? Isn't that in Egypt?" my friends asked in disbelief. "Why would you want to go there?"

Why indeed. Maybe it was watching *The Ten Commandments* in junior high school that got me started. Charlton Heston, as Moses in the court of the Pharaoh Rameses II, and Yul Brynner, who had played Rameses II, were both heartthrobs for me. The allure of the glamour of Egyptian royalty, like Nefertiri in the movie, with all those great costumes, was understandable. Or, did my desire to go to Cairo come from some deeper, hidden seed planted in past lifetimes? It never occurred to me that I could go there. My family rarely left town or went on vacations. We did not discuss international travel, senior trips, and certainly not Egypt.

I kept this desire stuffed down inside me. Somehow I knew Egypt had something special for me. Now, over thirty years after that high school confession, I had met Nicki who had real Egyptian adventures. The old desire bubbled up out of me again.

I soon had an opportunity to discover what Nicki had to offer. She was scheduled to teach a weekend class in Port Townsend, Washington, a beautiful old Victorian era town on the water's edge, full of wooden ships and delightful shops. It was an easy trip from Seattle so I signed up for the class. Between the time I met her in San Francisco in July and the class, which was in September, I had experienced the voice but had not yet developed the water altar. I would later look back on this weekend and realize it was another part of my initiation to the larger calling Spirit was inviting me to explore.

Going to Port Townsend from Seattle involved the ferry. I drove downtown after the morning rush hour, heading west to the water and the ferry dock. Dodging tourists clutching Starbucks coffees and pastries, I crossed over Alaskan Way into the parking area of Pier 52 for the Bremerton Ferry. Stopping at the ticket window I paid for my vehicle/driver fare, drove to the end of the line, and turned off the ignition. Waiting for the next boat, I enjoyed the latte I had brought with me and the beautiful view of the Olympic Mountains west of the wide Puget Sound waters. The previous ferry faded from view as it crossed the waters, sailing west to the Olympic Peninsula, a gentle wake following behind it. Soon the next ferry could be seen approaching us on its return trip, growing larger as it came closer. Finally it docked; the cars on it drove off one by one as they began their day in Seattle. After the last one cleared the loading area, we were allowed to drive our cars up the ramp and onto the deck. I always enjoyed the ferry but since I had been thinking about Hurricane Floyd and what that voice wanted of me, crossing over the waters was more meaningful. However, by the time we were docking in Port Townsend, thoughts of Floyd had faded and dreams of Egypt were taking over.

Driving to my motel to check in and get unpacked, I wondered about the weekend class. It was going to be about Sekhmet, the lion goddess of the ancient Egyptian pantheon. Nicki would be teaching us through shamanic journey work in which she would lead us in guided meditations to meet Sekhmet and receive her teachings. I was not too sure about all of it. It sounded a bit like a vision quest done from the comfort of a hotel meeting room. Well, I would just go along and see what happened.

When class convened we took time to share our backgrounds with each other and our intentions for being there to devote a weekend to Sekhmet. Nicki seemed very knowledgeable about this lioness as well as other members of the Egyptian pantheon. She explained that each of the *neteru*, as the gods and goddess were referred to, was an archetype of an ancient cosmology of wisdom. She said they were her teachers. The rest of the class seemed to be adepts at this kind of thing. They all talked about their trips to Egypt or the classes they had taken with Nicki. They shared their shamanic and visionary experiences with these Egyptian pantheonic beings as though they were best friends they hung out with.

I was feeling totally out of my league. Egyptian gods and goddesses as real people you can see and talk to? I still hadn't gotten used to the idea of the voice talking to me and now I am going to meet a lion goddess? I wasn't too sure about it.

Yet.

Our group was friendly; the setting beautiful. I tried to relax and not feel like I was the only one who didn't know what was going on. It came to the time in the class when Nicki would lead us on the guided journey to take us out to meet our Egyptian guide, Sekhmet. Everyone was settling down in their seats, some even lay down on the floor, acting like this was a routine they all knew.

I stayed seated in my chair, relaxing as best I could, following her instructions to deepen my breathing and to focus on my heartbeat. I was feeling skeptical, yet hopeful that this journey thing was something I could do. Where was I going to go? How would I get there? What was going to happen? Was it safe?

Hope prevailed.

My breath seemed to transport me. I found myself traveling along on the sound of Nicki's voice away from Port Townsend, away from what was familiar to me. I was no longer in the hotel room and had a sense of passing over water. I felt propelled toward some other place, some other time. Nicki's voice droned on in the background. It was like observing what she was saying, as if I was watching a movie unfolding in front of me. All of a sudden, a large bird—I mean very large—showed up and picked me up in its big, long beak! It was rather shocking, to say the least. I remember the image being something like the old children's story of a stork holding the baby in its blanket about to be delivered to the new mother. Nicki was saying something about Sekhmet and a temple. She was definitely not talking about this bird and I was not being told I was hanging from its beak! The great bird was intently peering at me through eyes that seemed to hold all of the cosmos in them. I felt oddly safe with this being; like I knew it—him. I trusted him. I didn't know what was going on but I knew it was happening. I just surrendered and hung from his beak, looking into his eyes.

Now Nicki was telling us to come back from the journey, back to present time and space. The bird was gone. I was sitting in my chair in the hotel room. I felt disoriented. Nicki was grinning, rubbing her hands together, excited as a kid with Christmas presents to open. She wanted to know what happened to us. Did we see Sekhmet? What did she say? People took turns sharing their experiences of the journey. Most said they had seen Sekhmet, had talked with her, or been in her temple in Egypt with her. With each story Nicki got more excited. She loved hearing what her students experienced. When it was my turn to share I said I never saw Sekhmet and didn't know who my guide was, but a great big stork came and picked me up in his beak like a baby!

Nicki stopped grinning. Leaning all the way forward in her chair, her eyes boring into me from across the room, she demanded:

"Was it a stork or an ibis?"

"I don't know," I replied, "what's the difference?"

The entire class was staring at me. I had a strange feeling that they all knew something I didn't.

"The ibis," Nicki said, "is my personal guide. My teacher. The ibis is Thoth, the Egyptian god of wisdom. Is that who you saw? What did he say to you?

Cosmic drumroll. Something changed in me.

"Well, it could have been an ibis. I'm not sure what one looks like. Anyway, this bird picked me up and told me I was his." I could hardly believe I was saying these things.

It seemed like a long time elapsed but I am sure it was only a few seconds. Sitting back in her chair, Nicki said, "Once Thoth claims you, that is it. You are his."

She moved on to the next person in the class to hear their journey experience. I just sat there. What had happened? Who is this Thoth? I belong to him now? What does that mean? What have I done?

What happened is that it was Thoth and he did claim me. (See plate 10 for a photo of Thoth from a temple wall in Abydos, Egypt.) That experience was the beginning of a whole new realm of studies for me. I enrolled in Nicki's Egyptian Mystery School as well as her Alchemical Healing classes that she taught from her home in Eugene, Oregon. I started making regular weekend trips of the six-hour drive from Seattle to Eugene with my new friend, Gloria Taylor Brown, whom I met at the Sekhmet class. Sometimes we were joined by other women who became friends and colleagues. We loaded up my Honda Odyssey minivan—the "Official Car of the Egyptian Mysteries"—and headed south, out of Seattle on I-5, driving to Nicki's house and cosmic realms beyond.

It was there that the deeper mysteries of the ancient Egyptian pantheon were revealed through her teachings and beautiful, heartfelt ceremonies. I learned more about the neteru. At first, I admit, I still balked over seeing and talking with these beings, but with each class my confidence and my ability to go out on shamanic journeys grew. While journeying I would experience a consciousness shift, finding myself in the world of ancient Egypt, communing with Isis, Anubis, Thoth, Sekhmet, and others of the pantheon. It was astounding. I experienced Technicolor visions, would receive teachings from my guides, and yet come out of the sessions crying, thinking that I did not see or learn anything at all. Nicki said I was a hard sell.

Yet, she was patient with me. Being a great teacher she gave me time to process, to trust in what was happening to me. I was learning the shamanic journey ways, learning to shift my consciousness into other realms and, with Thoth's guidance, connect with ancient wisdom, which I could bring back into my present life to use in healing work and my own advancement through study and commitment.

I remembered the experience at Hawkwind when I relived an ancient battle and pulled a sword from a woman's back. Reflecting on that event, hearing the voice, which led to creating the sacred water altar, and all I had been learning from Nicki, I reached a realization about myself. I wasn't ready to say, "I am a shaman," but I was willing to say, "I am available."

All of this led me to yet another life-changing event. At the end of a transformative weekend at Nicki's, I was standing in her living room looking at an Egyptian papyrus of a beautiful woman with a very long body full of stars, arching over the people below, covering them like the night sky. Her feet tiptoed to the ground, her arms and fingers reached downward, her breast hung pendulously as if heavy with milk. It seemed she outlined their world and protected them by her presence. Behind her was a field of stars on a dark blue background. A series of red disks were drawn from her mouth through her body. Her beauty touched a very deep place in my heart. I looked at this papyrus for a long time. A feeling of love arose in me. So did my tears. I needed to know who this woman was. I was about to go find Nicki to ask her when I realized she was standing next to me, silently sharing in this moment with me.

"Who is this, Nicki?"

"That is Nut, the mother of Isis and Osiris, Set and Nepthys. She is the Egyptian goddess of the Milky Way. See the red disks inside her body? That is Ra, the sun god. Nut swallows Ra at night, he travels through her body, then she gives birth to him in the morning."

We stared at this beautiful woman, this goddess. Nicki held my hand. She waited, allowing me the moment.

I turned to her. "Nicki. I have to go to Egypt."

21

Egypt 2001

WE BEGAN THE LONG DESCENT into Cairo as the sun was setting. From my window seat over the wing of the Egyptian Air jet, I could see the sun, Ra, a blazing red orb, directly in front of me as it, and our plane, crossed the western Egyptian sky. As the plane continued to drop down, slowing its speed, the great sun god pulled the daylight behind him, traveling in sync with us, lining up exactly on the tip of the plane wing and precisely tracking with the top of the wing, as we flew toward the airport. Our plane was sharing the passage of Ra's journey, being pulled to the same destination; into the body of Nut, the night sky. We were going home to Nut, home to Egypt. As we continued our descent, the sun stayed on the edge of the wing, getting smaller and smaller, and finally, in a single second, it disappeared from the wing into complete darkness. Ra had been pulled into Nut's mouth as she swallowed him. He was gone into the night mystery of her body. At that exact moment, we landed on the runway of the Cairo airport.

I sat in my seat, stunned. It was November 11, 2001.

For the past eight months I had been preparing for this trip; saving money, buying new luggage, making endless lists, arranging to be gone from my home and massage practice for three weeks, and sharing my excitement with anyone who would listen to me. Then September 11,

2001, happened. As the twin towers fell, the shock waves reverberated through all of us. Panic and fear spread like a virus. Egypt seemed very far away.

The chiropractor I worked with, my clients, friends, even my son were all assuming the trip would be cancelled. Thirty-three people, including me, were scheduled to fly out of our hometowns to meet in New York for our November 10 direct flight to Cairo. Now it seemed the whole world had changed. Something deep inside me told me to go. I admit I was worried, but I did not want to cancel my trip.

Over the past year of taking the Egyptian Mysteries classes with Nicki, I also committed to the training to become a certified instructor of Alchemical Healing, the shamanic healing method Nicki had developed over many years, taught to her by Thoth. I had learned to know Thoth as my own guide and teacher since that day in Port Townsend when he first claimed me as his own. To be an instructor of Alchemical Healing required mastery of the protocols, but also included a ceremony with Nicki acting as the direct link between Thoth and me. I was the initiate entering into his Alchemical Healing lineage. Thoth, being the keeper of the akashic records, the realm where all knowledge and activity is stored, would pass the archetypal wisdom, the alchemy of the work, through Nicki to me as a direct transmission of energy. This transmission would be like having a blueprint inscribed into my personal energy field, my etheric body.

It was an ordination. Unlike the Mormon religion, which restricted me, as a woman, from being a priesthood holder, this was a power I could receive and use to help others. Nicki had planned to perform the ceremony for me in Egypt, where it all started.

Now the 9/11 attacks had happened. Through the still-expanding grief and horror, the fear of traveling, especially by plane, and especially to a foreign nation, spread. People were just in so much shock. Still, I could not imagine not going on this trip. It had been over thirty-four years since that day in high school when I proclaimed my desire to go to Cairo. I wasn't ready to give up now. I waited a few days before I called Nicki. I asked her to be honest. Did she think it was safe for us to still go to Egypt? She told me she had been in almost constant communication with her dear friends who arranged her travel in Egypt— Mohammed Nazmy and Emil Shaker of Quest Tours, based in Giza. She assured me that if they didn't think it was safe they would tell her not to come. They were saying to come.

"So, Nicki, is the trip still on? Are we going?"

She replied by asking me, "Are you still in?"

"Absolutely," I assured her. "Are you still offering the tour?"

Nicki replied, "Even if it is just you and me, we are going."

And go we did. Our group turned out to be nine intrepid souls who packed our bags, braved the incredibly long lines through newly beefed up airport security, stared in amazement at never-before-seen armed guards in American airports, gripped our passports, and embarked on the long flight to Cairo. I was thrilled beyond my wildest hopes.

I was finally going to Egypt.

Wanting to do water altar ceremonies in Egypt, my luggage included five plastic bottles of elixir sealed in ziplock plastic bags. Even with all the increased security in those first months of post-9/11, passengers were still allowed to carry personal water bottles onto the planes. I felt as if those little bottles were the most precious cargo on board.

Egypt was magnificent. I loved it immediately. Each day was filled with magic, mystery, and awe as we visited the ancient sites and temples. The Egyptian people welcomed us as family. We were often greeted by them saying to us, "Welcome home." And, it felt like home. My special initiation ceremony was planned to occur early in the trip on Elephantine Island, at Aswan. We left Cairo, where we had our first view of the pyramids and had visited the Sphinx, and traveled by train south to Aswan, following the Nile upriver toward its source deep in Egypt. I found sleep nearly impossible on the train. I was so excited. This was Egypt! I could sleep when I got home.

Aswan was beautiful. Its sky was cleaner than smog-ridden Cairo, and the city was less populated. Aswan was also our first opportunity to be on the Nile. So far, our travel had all been on land with only momentary glimpses of the great river of life that flows through Egypt. (See plate 11 for a photo of sunrise at Aswan.)

The day of my ceremony dawned very early. I dressed in a long, white, cotton robe embroidered with beautiful designs, called a *galabia*. Nicki let me wear one of her necklaces adorned with a huge glass bead she had crafted with her jewelry torch back in Eugene. A long black scarf flowed from under my wide-brimmed hat and down my shoulders. My fellow travelers all knew what the day held for me. We spoke very little, honoring the occasion. A smile or a squeeze of a hand let me know they were supportive of me. A feeling of love and grace surrounded us as we walked the short distance from our hotel to the dock, stepped into the small sailing boat, called a *felucca,* which was waiting to take us across the Nile from Aswan to Elephantine Island.

I felt like a priestess who had returned from afar, reunited with her homeland. Time seemed to slow down. The sun on my skin felt like a personal blessing from Ra. I trailed my hand over the side of the boat, feeling the ancient water of the Nile flow through my fingers, watching the drops fall off of me and blend back into the river. As we got closer to the island, smells of ancient land and rocks wafted up in the heat of the day. The power of this land tangibly shimmered around ancient statues and bright flowers.

We disembarked and walked up timeworn stone stairs onto the island, each step a reconnection to a timeless bond between me and Egypt. My soul remembered this place. My heart rejoiced to be home again as we walked through layers of ruins of ancient buildings erected on top of one another over centuries of living, now partially exposed from excavations. Mysteries and secrets of long forgotten people hung over the island like ghosts, waiting to tell their stories to those who could listen and hear.

Finally we arrived at what used to be the temple of Khnum, the ram-headed creator god who sat at the cosmic potter's wheel molding life from clay. One story of Khnum portrays him as the god who made the cosmic egg from which Ra was born. Khnum is also revered as a Nile River god. Nicki had chosen this site to perform my lineage transmission ceremony. It seemed appropriate for the water priestess to come to the Nile, the source of life, for this day of rebirth. (See plates 12 and 13 for photos of the ceremony.)

Khnum's temple was now mostly rubble, but two columns remained. Inscribed with still-visible images of Thoth, the columns framed a large stone altar that stood intact amidst the crumbled ruins. We silently approached the altar. I laid my hands on it. It was hot from absorbing the sun's rays. We all arranged our personal ritual items on it, preparing for ceremony. As I placed one of the bottles of elixir on it, I wondered how many centuries of ceremony that ancient stone had supported. For a moment I felt the presence of my own altar room thousands of miles away. A deep feeling of connection to this place spread through me. It was late afternoon. The air was cooling to a pleasant temperature. The light would be gone soon. Magic was in the air.

Nicki and I stood in front of the altar. We smudged each other and the rest of the group, who had circled around us as sacred witnesses. It was my moment.

Facing me, Nicki anointed my forehead with Egyptian oil she had purchased, especially for this ceremony, from a shopkeeper in Giza, near the Sphinx. Holding my hands, she smiled and told me to see Thoth. I took a deep breath and exhaled. Again I inhaled, pulling into me the smells of the hot Egyptian dirt and stones, the dry air, the exquisite aroma of the Egyptian oil on my face. I exhaled and looked at Nicki, seeing the face I had grown to love as a teacher, mentor, and friend. The outlines of her features blurred, the ground under my feet, and the air around me seemed to shift and move. Waves of energy flowed through me. A strong but quiet sense of power settled around us. It was totally silent. As I stood there watching Nicki, the form of another being stepped into her and looked out at me through her eyes.

It was Thoth. I saw him shift into Nicki.

He became fully alive and present in her, looking at me through her eyes, holding me in his gaze. While Thoth watched, Nicki was speaking, calling in the ritual of this lineage transmission. I do not remember the words; perhaps I never even heard them. She was reaching inside of me, opening my chakras one by one, pulling out strands of my essence. I felt her pull them out like threads stretching from deep within me. Grasping the threads in her hand, she would lift her arm above her head, offering them to Thoth who would take them from her into his heart and mind, energizing them, infusing them with his own essence before handing them back to Nicki, who would reinsert them into me. She was the weaver; tying me into the ancient lineage, awakening old memories of having done this before, connecting me to Thoth, to her, and to the Alchemical Healing lineage. The power of Egypt surged through my body like electricity running through wires. With each chakra Nicki opened, more of that power filled me, anchoring me deep in the ancient dirt, stones, and water that flowed as the Nile beneath the island, but also lifting me up, expanding me into an ancient, cosmic connection. The sun was fading; shadows began to creep across the altar. The call for evening prayer from the Aswan Muslim temples floated across the water. It was the time of prayer. Many of the local population would be lifting their voices right now to Allah.

Nicki kept weaving the ancient patterns through me. Thoth held me enthralled, staring at me. Nicki reached my third eye. As she touched me and reached inside of it a great ruby ignited and blazed in my forehead. I felt the connection to the ancient ones of Egypt come alive inside me, all the adepts who had carried on the mystery school traditions through the ages, all who sought the wisdom, all who were connected to Thoth. It was more than a spiritual lineage. I felt it alive inside my cells—a genetic memory. The power surged through me, jolting me. With ruby blazing, my hands vibrating with the sacred power, my chakras fully awakened and connected to Thoth, I became a sacred transmitter both receiving and broadcasting. A priestess to the mysteries, back in the temple built above the Nile.

As Nicki passed her hands up to the top of my head, the power was flowing through me like a wild river. I became a fountain, energy gushing like water up through my feet, coursing through my entire body, flowing out of my hands. And then, in the final moments of the transmission, came a totally unexpected and shocking revelation. I saw my father standing with Thoth.

"Daddy? What are you doing here? You know Thoth?"

His answer to me was the great feeling of pride a father has for his daughter who has achieved more than he could have expected of her. There was no breach of religion or belief between us. We had never reached this level of understanding while he was alive and yet, here he was at this incredible moment. Tears flowed down my face as I looked into the faces of Nicki, Thoth, and my father. Deep love surrounded me. In that moment, I knew I had truly stepped into my destiny.

It was almost dark. The ceremony was completed. The group welcomed me back into their midst with hugs, smiles, and tears. Not wanting to walk through those ruins in the darkness, we quickly prepared to leave, gathering our things from the altar. I kept the bottle of elixir in my hand. In silence we made our way down the hill to our boat, which had come around the back side of the island to wait for us. At the water's edge I stopped. Lifting the elixir up as an offering, I gave thanks to the ancient ones of Egypt, to my father, for the ceremony just completed, and for my new place in the lineage of Thoth. As darkness fell, I poured the elixir into the water. An amethyst shimmer fell from the bottle and flowed out across the Nile. (See plate 14 for a photo of the amethyst-colored water of the Nile.)

22

Water for Egypt

THE NEXT DAY WE VISITED the Temple of Isis at Philae, also on an island near Aswan. As we boarded our felucca the mood was very different from our previous outing. Everyone was laughing, talking, and generally in a joyful state of celebration. Nubian boatmen, dressed in colorful robes, sang and played drums for us as we sailed down the Nile. Heaps of Egyptian jewelry were passed around for us to admire and purchase. The sun sparkled off the Nile. We were told the river was very polluted but to me it looked beautiful, flowing through reeded areas where graceful, white egrets stood patiently waiting to grab fish with their long beaks. I thought of the elixir I had released into the river the night before and imagined streaks of amethyst circulating in the water.

We docked at Philae. Our boatmen assisted us out of the felucca onto stone stairs rising up to the temple complex. Stepping off the top stair onto the wide stones of the outer courtyard, I was jolted into a different consciousness. My feet sank deep into the ground, anchoring me, as my body grew and soared up above the high porticoes of the temple. I felt over 100 feet tall. A deep knowing that I belonged there, that I had been there before, filled me.

A powerful voice within me cried out, "I am back!"

Shifting back into a more normal size, I joined the others in

The Temple of Isis at Philae
(See plates 15 and 16 for more photographs of this temple.)

experiencing the beautiful colonnades, their lovely fluted tops graced with lotus blossoms. Huge pylons rose into the blue sky. From the stone wall Isis smiled out at us, welcoming us. We passed through the portal to the inner court, the hypostyle hall, where ten huge columns stood. Faded now, they once were brightly painted to depict the first trees, flowers, and plants to grow up from the primeval mound of earth, represented by the temple floor. Looking up at the ceiling, faded vultures still flew in the ancient sky.

We were truly on sacred ground.

Continuing through the temple we reached the innermost sanctuary, the holy of holies, where the stone altar of Isis awaited us and the ceremony we had prepared to honor the great mother-goddess Isis and the elements of life that sustain us. Deep, prevailing love flowed through me. I approached the altar with awe, reverently touching the smooth, cool stone. We placed our personal items on the altar, as well as those that would represent the elements.

Earth. For Egypt, the ancient land of mystery; for our bodies, our ancestors; for the gift of wisdom and the giveaway of all of life that sustains us—someone set out a beautiful crystal.

Air. For our breath and prayers, for intention, inspiration; for new beginnings and rebirth—another person shared a white egret feather they had found by the river.

Fire. For the life force and passion, for courage and truth; for relationships and being mirrors for one another—a single candle was lit.

Water. For the sacred flow of all things, the eternally changing river that carries us each through our lives, connecting us to everyone and everything—the elixir was placed. Nicki and I had shopped in the souk the night before, searching for a vessel to hold the water for this ceremony. We purchased a small, white alabaster bowl that I now placed on the altar and filled with the elixir. I had to look twice. Water from my sacred water altar was sitting on the stone altar of Isis's temple in Egypt. Through the fury of Floyd, the waters of Spirit had flowed to Greenlake in Seattle, into my water altar, across the oceans, and into this holy temple. I felt blessed. Amazed.

We circled around the altar, honored for the privilege to do ceremony at this ancient, holy place. Our prayers to Isis sprang out through our hearts, across the altar, flowed into the Nile, and spread out across Egypt. Spirit was with us as a deep, loving presence; filling us with peace, joy, and gratitude.

Months ago in Eugene, I had told Nicki about the sacred water altar. She honored me as a teacher of this work, asking me to share the process with her so she could also become a water altar keeper. We had looked forward to sharing prayers for the waters and now here we were

The Goddess Isis

in Egypt together. We both knew that knowledge without application of it to benefit others and our Mother Earth was wasted; that teaching and ceremony are not about the ego and telling people how much we knew. It was the honoring and giving back that really mattered.

After a blissful time we left the sanctuary to explore the temple grounds. Philae, being on an island, is surrounded by the waters of the river. Throughout this trip we were also surrounded by guards with very big guns to be sure we were perfectly safe. They were always close by but allowed us free movement around the complex. Nicki and I walked to the back side of the temple following the sloping stones down to the edge of the Nile. No one else had come this way. We sat down and prayed for a long time there at the waters of life—the Nile. We cried for the people who had lost their lives in the 9/11 attacks. We cried for the fear and terror that now gripped so many people and prayed for that fear to turn to love and understanding; for darkness to turn to light. We cried in joy for being in Egypt and feeling the love of Isis, Thoth, and all the great ones of the ancient pantheon. We each held a bottle of elixir. Removing the lids, we poured the water into the Nile, watching it join the ancient flow as it coursed through Egypt.

When we finally got up and turned back toward the temple, I was surprised to see two machine-gun-toting guards leaning against a wall. They had been watching over us the whole time. I wonder what they thought of these two American women crying, praying, and pouring water from bottles with purple labels into the Nile. They never stopped us. I think they must have seen two ancient priestesses who had returned to the temple for a sacred ceremony. I think they blessed us.

Later in the tour we were given a special and surprise treat. As thanks for coming to Egypt when almost all tourists had stayed home, Nicki's friends at Quest Tours had arranged for us to have a complimentary stay at a brand-new Oberoi Hotels resort called the Sahl Hasheesh at Hurghada, on the Red Sea. Other than our little group there was only one other guest. We had the whole place to ourselves! It was luxury beyond anything I have ever experienced.

On a day spent lazing at the pool or snorkeling the coral reefs, Nicki and I took time out to again honor the waters. We waded out about waist deep, maybe 20 feet from the shore. I was astounded to be standing in the Red Sea. This whole trip had been one miracle after another. Taking the last two bottles of the sacred water altar elixir, we joined hands and prayers in thanks to the water for its gift of life, to the Nile and the Red Sea for keeping the land alive, for the waters of the earth and the waters of our bodies, and for the spiritual flow that keeps us connected with our guides and higher purpose. Deeply immersed in gratitude, we poured the elixir into the Red Sea. A vision formed in front of me. I clearly saw a large grizzly bear standing in a flowing mountain river grabbing a big salmon in her mouth! I told Nicki.

"You saw what?"

"A bear—a grizzly bear. It was just out there." I pointed to the place in front of me where I had seen the vision. "The salmon were swimming upstream and the bear was standing in the river. She grabbed a fat one and had it in her mouth!"

Nicki was silent for a moment, staring out in front of her. Then she turned to face me. "You have seen the joining of the Red Sea and the waters of the Pacific Northwest from home," she exclaimed. "Our work here has joined the waters."

Feeling that connection between our homes in Washington and Oregon and our ancient home of Egypt, I was at peace. My journey with the sacred water altar led me here, to Egypt. I filled the now empty elixir bottles with water from the Red Sea. I would take it home with me to join the contents of a large glass punch bowl with an amethyst in it, sitting on an altar in a condo in Seattle. I knew that soon after I returned home I would be walking in the moonlight along the shore of Puget Sound where I would release that precious blend into the waters, completing the cycle.

23

Journey

Nut and the Nile

THE NILE

THE NILE, THE LONGEST of Earth's rivers, flows through the Egyptian desert transporting us through centuries of history and mystery. Prior to the building of the Aswan High Dam in the 1960s, the Nile was wild and free-flowing, full of crocodiles and mystery. Throughout Egyptian history the most important event of the year was the *inundation*, or flooding, of the Nile, which brought the fullness of the river and deposits of rich dirt, ensuring a successful agricultural season. The ancient Egyptian calendar started with this event, correlated with the summer solstice, and the rising of the star Sirius, seen by the ancient Egyptians as Isis. It was a time of return to life after the dormant winter when food stores and the river were running low. If the Nile failed to flood and bring its lifeblood of water and precious top soils, the coming year would be hard indeed. Ancient traditions of honoring the gods and goddesses of the Nile are numerous. The river was essential to life and was honored by erecting temples close to its banks. Even today the Nile is essential to all Egyptians. Where the water flows the land is rich, black, and fertile making a distinct line where the dry desert goes without it.

Egrets on the Nile

NUT

The goddess Nut is the great cosmic mother. Her form is the Milky Way bending over the Earth. Each night she swallows Ra, the sun, and gives birth to him again each morning after his night passage through her body. She is thus a symbol of death and rebirth. The ancient Egyptians depicted her body full of five-pointed stars, representing her human children as star seeds born to earth and destined to return to the divine home she holds for us. She is said to receive all her children back into her body when death occurs and is depicted on coffin lids and tomb ceilings across Egypt. Nut is the mother of Nepthys and Set, Osiris and Isis, who brings the inundation. The ancient law of As Above, So Below, is perfectly expressed in the relationship between Nut and the Nile. The ancient ones believed the Nile was the reflected body of Nut on earth, spreading out across the desert lands of Egypt, bringing life, just as Nut spread out across the sky, giving life to her children and receiving them back into her body when the journey was over.

☀ Intention

Our intention for this journey is to be with the Nile during its inundation and experience a spiritual and personal renewal. Where in your life do you feel the need for renewal? What qualities do you desire to rise within you? Where do you feel the need for restoration? Where have you been depleted and desire a rebirth? How do you offer reciprocity in your life? What new seeds are you ready to plant to flourish within you?

Feel your breath within you and allow it to grow; each breath more full and expansive than the last. Breathe in. Feel the expansion of your chest and lungs. Breathe out, releasing the spent

The Goddess Nut (Illustration by Patricia Catlett)

energy within you. Breathe in. Fill yourself with the river of life-giving oxygen flowing into you. Breathe out, releasing the old, anticipating the new to come into you.

You are walking along the shore of the Nile. The water level is low, leaving large areas of exposed land pocked with mud. A lingering odor of dead fish prevails, making you long for the fresh smell of running water. There is a general feeling of depletion within you; of long waiting to be filled with newness, to feel the regeneration of your life, your purpose, your reserves. As you walk along, you see waterbirds poking expectantly in the mud looking for any remains they might glean. The fields behind you are empty. Children are quiet in the heat, women prepare a meager meal with the last remains of the winter stores. Old men sit idly watching the river. Everyone seems to be waiting . . . waiting on the river.

You hear your name called out. Someone is hailing you from a boat on the river, far out in front of you. You see some boards stretched out to reach the water's edge and walk to them. Stepping onto them, you cross the mud and swampy area out to the flowing part of the river. You reach the boat where a guide waits for you and invites you on a journey. Feeling safe and somehow knowing your desire for change has been heard, you accept your guide's invitation and assistance in getting into the boat.

You settle into your seat as your guide pushes away from the shallow edge and enters into the larger flow of the Nile. Notice the scenes on and around the river, the sunlight shining on the water. White egrets sit atop clumps of water lilies. An occasional cow swims from shore to a small island, looking for any remaining grass to eat. Birds fly overhead. Even in the time of low waters life flows here. You feel the joy of being on the river; being carried along its life-giving flow.

As you watch the scenery change in front of you, you notice the growing image of a building downstream. As you get closer you see it is a temple. You can see the wide portico with its columns reaching high into the Egyptian sky. Seeing this temple gives you a feeling of familiarity, as if you have been there before. Happiness and excitement grow in you as the boat brings you closer and closer to the temple.

Your guide steers the boat into a docking area that is flooded with water for access. Steep stone steps rise out of the water and up to the temple grounds. Your guide secures the boat and helps you out onto the stairs. You begin to walk up. How does it feel to be walking up these stairs toward this temple? Notice how you look. What are you wearing?

As you step onto the stones of the temple courtyard, notice your surroundings—the tall columns painted with rich colors and glyphs, brightly painted scenes of people drawing water from the river, animals drinking at the river's edge, crocodiles half submerged in the water, ducks, flowers, and images of the goddess Isis. Notice the beauty of the temple. This temple was built to honor the river—the Nile—to honor Isis and the inundation.

Enjoying the beauty around you, you cross the courtyard and enter into the temple. It is cool inside, out of the bright sunlight. A feeling of sacredness and peace permeates the stone walls and floors. You are welcomed by an attendant who will help prepare you for further access to the temple. You are taken to a side room and given water to wash with, perfumed oil for your skin, and beautiful robes to wear. You are left alone to ready yourself.

The attendant returns and leads you out of the room into the inner sanctuary where a beautiful altar sits softly aglow with candles. The floor beneath the altar is painted to show the black dirt of Egypt with the Nile flowing through it, flowing through this sanctuary. Looking up you see the ceiling has been richly painted with a field of stars. More than stars; it is Nut, mother of Isis, cosmic mother to all. Her starry form bends over the ceiling, arms and legs reaching down to the floor. Her beautiful face serenely watching you. You are filled with a great sense of love, of hope.

The attendant leaves and you are left alone. You approach the altar ready to make offerings to the Nile, to Isis, to Nut. You have

The Nile

come to offer that which is depleted in you, that which is dead, that which is wanting in you. You know that by offering these things here, at this sacred place, they will be taken from you; that the Nile, Isis, and Nut will bring you restoration and renewal. Feeling this hope in your heart, you pour your offerings onto the altar like water, like tears flowing from you. And you pray for your restoration, for renewal, for a new beginning.

The candles on the altar flicker from a faint breeze. Turning toward the breeze you notice a stairway at the back of the sanctuary. You feel drawn to go to the stairs. Leaving the altar you walk to them. They lead down. Light shimmers around the steps—the light of the sun shining off water. You can smell the water close by and realize these steps will lead you down to the river, to the Nile.

Placing your hand on a graceful railing, you walk down stone stairs. They feel cool beneath your feet. It is only a short distance until you step off the bottom stair. In front of you is a beautiful pool, rimmed with precious gold and made of finely carved crystals and jewels. You stand in amazement looking at this beautiful pool. The waters of the Nile flow into it; it is deep enough to float in. Once again you offer your prayers to the river, to Isis, and to Nut asking for the blessing of the inundation—for the flow of abundance and all good things to return.

You step into the pool now, the water flowing over your body. You float, supported by the Nile that brings life to Egypt. You feel your worries drop away from you. Feel a great sense of peace, of calm. Let the water soothe you. Let the water hold you.

You begin to notice an incredible, delicate, and amazing scent. It fills the chamber and floods your senses. A primeval essence of purity, bliss, it seems to permeate every cell of your body. Where is this scent coming from?

Out of the water rises a lotus. A pure white flower emitting this heavenly aroma, it shines in its own light, radiant. It rises from the depths of the river below where the old and cast-off parts of life have settled, rotted, and become the fertile womb for this amazing flower. You remember your offerings at the altar—what you cast off that no longer gave you life, no longer fed you, and, like the bottom mud of the Nile, became the food for renewal, for blossoming.

You can see the stems of the lotus in the water below, rising up, strong, resilient, providing the structure and support for the precious flower that now rests on the water. You think about the structure in your life that supports what is beautiful in you.

The broad leaves of the lotus reach out to you, inviting you to become a part of it. This divine beauty wants to hold you, support you. You raise yourself out of the water and onto the leaves of the lotus, feeling its strength, its support. You settle yourself and lay back on the lotus, feeling the grace of the Nile that provides this life, this beauty. The aroma of the flower seems to lift you. You are part of the blossom now, unfolding in beauty, perfection.

As you lay on the lotus you feel the waters below you begin to rise. The water level is becoming higher in the pool. The inundation has occurred! Gently the waters rise in the pool, overflowing it, filling the entire chamber. You rise up and up on the lotus. You rise up and out of the temple. You rise up and into the night sky until you are floating in the stars. There, above you, is Nut, the great sky mother, stretched out over you, protecting you. You are her star-seed child, living and experiencing the earthly realm. Feel yourself held in the starry womb of Nut, ever connected to her. Feel yourself nourished and fed, renewed by her love and eternal nurturing. She is there to guide you, to help you. Talk to Nut. Feel her love. Listen to what she tells you.

The night sky dims. The shape of Nut begins to fade. Before her figure is gone, you see the first light of the sun coming out of the night; Ra emerging from the body of Nut as she gives birth to a new day. Ra rises, his rays reaching out across the sky. You feel the dawn within you, the awakening you have prayed for, waited for. You rejoice in this new beginning.

As Ra fills the sky you gently drift back to stand next to the Nile. Your feet grounded on the rich Egyptian soil, like the topsoil newly deposited by the Nile, you are ready to be planted with the seeds of a new beginning. Full of gratitude you want to offer gifts to the river, to Isis, and to Nut. What gifts do you give? See your gifts accepted.

Nut has left a gift for you with the Nile. It is rising up out of the water now. Reach out and accept your gift. What is it Nut has given to you?

Taking a last look around you, you realize it is time for you to return now. Return to your life richly renewed, knowing that you can return to Nut and the Nile when you need to, when you want to. But now, focus on your breath. Breathing in. Breathing out. Feel your body. You are back in this time and space. Breathing in. Breathing out. You are filled with the inundation of Spirit, with the blessings of Nut.

24

Water for Peace

IN FEBRUARY 2003, I taught a workshop on creating sacred water altars at the Seattle Women of Wisdom (WOW) conference. This ten-day event featured nationally known keynote speakers presenting their expertise in areas of women's spirituality. The WOW Board of Directors, all wise women themselves, also drew on the deep well of richly talented local women to present workshops, musical offerings, and art. I felt honored to have my workshop accepted. WOW had become an annual event for me. It was more than a conference; it was community, a reunion of friends and spiritual family that met once a year.

The class was successful and the women attending it seemed genuinely interested in going home to make their own sacred water altars. I was happy to be teaching this work given to me by Spirit. I trusted I was making a difference for the water.

One evening as I was getting ready to leave, my friend Gloria Taylor Brown, who was also on the WOW Board, hurried up to me, telling me there was someone I had to meet.

"Who is it?" I asked.

"I don't know his name," Gloria said, "but he has special water labels. You have to go see him. He is downstairs in the vendors' area."

Curious, I went to see. His name was Michael "Buffalo" Mazzetti, and his company, the Okanagon Highlands Bottling Company, was based in eastern Washington. Originating from political action, they had created a water-bottle label to bring awareness to change the Federal Mining Law of 1872, which still sells our national forests for five dollars per acre. The label proclaimed, "Water is more precious than gold!"

Over time I developed a relationship with the company and decided to "put my money where my mouth is." Using OHBC's connections, I put up the money and the design idea to have a new label created for water bottles, which was then to be distributed by the OHBC. The label was called, Water for Peace. One side of the label was dedicated to the OHBC's political agenda, urging people to write letters to Washington requesting then-President George Bush to end the Gulf War. My side of the label was spiritual in nature. I had these words printed, "Focus on Peace. Drink Water. Think Peace. Take Action. Change the World. Thank you, Water, for your gift of life. I see you clean and restored. I am at peace."

The professionally created label turned out beautifully. On a deep purple background was a picture of a woman pouring water from a jug with a peace sign on it, sparkling blue streams of water flowing out of the jug and across the label. The image of the woman was fashioned after the art work of Alphonse Mucha, my favorite artist.

Mucha's art, from the late 1800s and early 1900s, is in the Art Nouveau period. While he produced a wide variety of art, sculpture, and jewelry, he is probably most known for the many beautiful women he painted. I attended a rare exhibit of his art one full-moon evening in Seattle. The paintings seemed to be alive, the women in them all radiated beauty and a sense of divine feminine. Two paintings were especially captivating to me. One was Mucha's self-portrait, the other his wife. The museum had displayed them on the floor, side by side. They were so luminous I thought they had been set up with some kind of backlighting. Curious, I walked behind the paintings to see how this effect had been created. To my amazement, there was nothing behind them. The glow came from the paintings, as if Mucha had painted with light.

Continuing through the exhibit, I came face to face with his bronze sculpture *Nature,* a perfectly sculpted bust of a woman. Her eyes were closed, as if at rest, her face delicate and shining. Long, flowing hair cascaded from under an intricately carved crown, cascaded down her shoulders, wrapped around her breasts, and turned into the base of the sculpture. From the top of the crown she wore, emerging just above what would be the third eye, a very large amethyst egg rested on an elaborate flowerlike pedestal. Standing in front of this magnificent creation was, to me, like seeing Gaia herself. I felt deeply connected to the beauty of our Mother, the beauty of life. Overwhelmed, I wept. I was reminded of the high vibrational qualities of amethyst. It had come to me for the water altar and now here it was again in this incredible statute *Nature.*

That experience continued to influence me. I obtained a picture of the statue, framed it, and placed it in the altar room, next to the water altar. As I was thinking about the design for the Water for Peace label, it seemed right to honor what I saw as Gaia, with her crown holding an amethyst egg.

I saw the creation of the Water for Peace label as an opportunity to put a little spirituality on the supermarket shelves. Each part of the label had carefully planned symbolism designed into it. The Mucha-influenced woman, Gaia, wears a delicate crescent moon necklace, which is the Alchemical Healing symbol for water. She is surrounded by a circle of stars. Her action of pouring water from a jug is reminiscent of the celestial woman often seen in images portraying the water carrier of the astrological sign of Aquarius, pouring the waters of Spirit out for all to receive. Of course, the peace sign is universal. The entire project was inspired by the sacred water altar and the homemade labels I created. Since I used purple paper for my own labels, I had to have this label infused with a deep amethyst purple as well. I enjoyed layering the Water for Peace label with different symbols, knowing some people would get it and others would not.

When the first printing of the labels ended up on actual bottles of water to be sold in retail stores I was overjoyed. The sacred water altar had expanded out into the public! Unfortunately, the OHBC was unable to make a strong marketing push with Water for Peace and it never made it into the mainstream stores. It was sold at small stores that wanted to support the project. While not a commercial success, I felt satisfied that I had created this label whose beauty and words of peace permeated thousands of bottles of water.

Thank you, Water, for your gift of life. I see you clean and restored.

Water for Peace label

25

Cosmic Recycling

AS A YOUNG GIRL I loved to lie on the ground warmed by the summer sun, enjoying a timeless activity innate in humans—cloud watching. We have all delighted in perusing the picture-book of the sky, its vaporous volumes full of endless possibilities. With no lack of cumulus plots to investigate, I spent hours delighting in this activity, imagining great celestial ships sailing across the sea of blue sky to disappear over the horizon, or a dragon's puffy talons reaching out to grab me.

On one of these occasions, nestled in the sweet-smelling grass of our front yard, I allowed my curiosity to drift from the sky toward the ground, observing the rest of my surroundings: the neighbor's sprinkler tossing water onto their flower beds, a bird singing nearby, the leafy plumage of our mountain ash tree. At that moment it was as if I had never seen a tree before. Perhaps my perspective had become distorted after gazing upward for so long, but it seemed to me that I, the tree, and all I observed were underground, part of a secret realm unknown to anyone but me. This was better than cloud watching! I had discovered a new world. If all I could see in my field of view was the underworld, then the tree roots hidden beneath the grassy lawn must be pushing out into the sky of another realm where unknown beings, perhaps not unlike this human child, spent their time watching gnarly limbs outline the sky of their existence.

The image of this world reversal was profound for a girl of eight or nine years. That tree was teaching me, inviting me to explore the microcosmic nature of the life around me. The ageless concept, As Above, So Below, was evident in my seeing the tree and my world upside down. Trees do indeed exist above and below ground, interconnecting the two realms. I thought if I could crawl inside one, it would be like riding in an elevator moving me from one level to the other, transporting me while I stood still.

The fact is, trees have a lot to do with movement. They are the great recyclers of life. They transpire it.

Transpiration is the circulation of water through trees. It is easy to be fooled by trees. Their woody bodies appear dense and compact but flowing inside are vertical rivers. More like living pumps than elevators, trees move water from below to above and back in a continuous cycle. The leaves of trees release water from special cells, called *stomates,* into the air around them. The ensuing evaporation creates a negative pressure in the surrounding cells of the trees. Wanting to neutralize the pressure, water is then pulled from the vascular tissues, the *xylem,* replacing the water in the leaves. This tension and resulting pulling extends all the way down the tree trunk to its roots, which constantly seek out groundwater to satisfy the pulling for more water.

A single mature tree can absorb carbon dioxide from the air around it at a rate of about 48 pounds per year. In return, it gives back nearly 260 pounds of oxygen—enough for two adult humans to breathe in a year. Trees not only give us oxygen, their watery breath is a major factor in bringing rain. As they exhale, water vapor collects around them, attracting existing moisture in the nearby air to join in their misty celebration. As more vapor collects, the air around the trees cools, allowing water in clouds above to come closer. Less heat means more water is able to fall through the atmosphere where it manifests as rain, fog, snow, or in other forms depending on existing atmospheric conditions.

Tree experts estimate that about 90 percent of the water taken in by a tree will be released back into the air as water vapor. A 350-foot redwood tree can move about 500 gallons of water a day; a single maple tree, in the summer, might pump as much as 50 gallons of water per hour. Transpiration, along with normal evaporation of water on land, makes up perhaps two-thirds of the moisture in the atmosphere, compared to evaporation over the oceans' surface, which is only one-third. Clearly trees are an integral link to water.

Trees stand together in forests, collectively transpiring and supporting Earth's incredible ecosystem. Their limbs create shade, keeping the air and ground cooled from the constant heat of the sun. Welcoming tree arms gather precipitation, allowing it to slowly drip through their fragrant leaves or needles, freshening and cleaning the air. The lungs of the Earth, the rain forests once covered as much as 14 percent of the Earth's land surface. Now, due to devastation and destruction caused by humans at the rate of around $1^1/_2$ acres every second, they occupy only about 6 percent. At that rate, the rest could be gone in forty years—if we could live that long without the trees. The magnificent California redwoods have only about 5 percent of their old-growth stands remaining.

Where trees have been destroyed by clear-cutting or after massive fires, the ground is exposed and no longer protected by the great Standing People. Water has no opportunity to trickle through branches, gently falling to the ground to be slowly percolated back into the soil. Instead it hits the ground running, causing erosion that strips away precious topsoil and all that lives upon it. The loss of trees also means the loss of transpiration and reduces the amount of water being recycled in an area. If enough trees are lost, deserts appear.

The constant process of transpiration recycles the Earth's waters. Gaia is not making new water every day; the existing supply just gets passed around. Stored in the oceans, rivers, aquifers, bodies of animals and plants, and in clouds, this lifeblood moves around the planet. Water re-collects. It remembers itself. As it moves around the Earth, in and out of every living cell, it collects, carries, pours out, and joins all of life; making it the collective consciousness of which we are each a drop in that sacred flow. The water I drink today might remember falling as rain on the Sphinx ten thousand years ago, when Egypt was a lush paradise. Maybe my bathwater allows me to immerse myself in the memory of whales singing to each other.

Due to their watery nature, trees also hold memory. Etched into every tree are the recordings of their annual growth and the conditions in which the tree has lived. Years of ample rain, times of drought, even if a tree was crowded on one side by growing too closely against a woody neighbor, all these nuances are dutifully recorded in the concentric, circular patterns of tree rings.

Tree rings are much like old phonograph records that were recorded, or cut, by way of an imprinting process that captured sound in deeply grooved circles. The process is the same whether the resulting audio is Led Zeppelin, Beethoven, or the chanting of Buddhist monks. The circular disk is the record; the recording of the moment is the memory. As the record spins on a turntable, a needle, or stylus, is placed in the groove, pin-pointing and releasing every sound that occurred during the recording process. We hear the memory of that process. In a recording session, any background noise in the studio is captured along with the artist's song or symphony offering. That is why sound booths protect the recording session from outside noise. Unlike that studio, trees do not filter out what they record. In addition to their own growth conditions, the trees also record the passage of water moving through them, laying down its fluid memory, imprinting the flow of time into their circular rings. The recordings in the trees, the memories, are then anchored into the earth by the roots of the trees.

Are there tree rings in North Carolina holding the memory of the screams of drowning pigs? Do the trees remember Floyd, dark inner circles marking forever the trauma of its passage?

When trees are ripped up during intense storms and hurricanes their roots no longer anchor their memories into Gaia. What happens to those memories? Separated from the tree, ripped out of the land, are they suddenly released into the flow of the storm? As the trees are bro-

Tree rings in the Hoh Rain Forest, Washington

ken apart and hurled along flooding rivers their porous bodies become saturated by the storm water. Water washes through their delicate rings, further releasing their tree memories back into the water. With so many violent storms occurring at record levels around the world it seems the Earth is being flooded with her own memories.

Water is the universal solvent; it carries within it a part of everything it passes through. The essence of cedar oil gleaned from raindrops falling in a forest mixes in with the sewage from washed out factory farms. It all goes into the water. Since water is constantly being recycled, it seems that after flowing around the earth and through all life upon it, being a part of all the activities and experiences throughout time, absorbing toxins and teardrops, its capacity for memory would be replete.

Fortunately, Gaia has provided a remedy for this. The natural purification of water is as timeless as water flowing. Water slowly passes through a simple yet perfect system. It percolates through the filter of the ground it passes through. It hangs out in porous rocks that either heat or cool it. Underground rivers transport it allowing impurities to be absorbed by various minerals in the soil, which purify, restore, and transform them. Water might spend a few millennia being formed into new rock through the crystallization process. Water finds its way aboveground through springs, wells, and geysers; seeping, bubbling, or gushing back to the surface. The fast-flowing motion of a river pulls oxygen through the water to help purify it, as does the sunlight shining down into it, creating dazzling diamond arrays to verify its presence. A wild river will meander and bend, forming oxbow lakes where the water circles around and can slow down, perhaps like a therapy pool, where it sorts out all the confusion and chaos and lets things settle where they may before rejoining the flow. Perhaps the river or stream takes a plunge over the side of a mountain in a beautiful, cascading waterfall. This falling and mixing with oxygen provides further purification. Eventually, all water returns to the ocean where it is remixed in the salty brine of the Earth's watery womb. Evaporation creates the reunion of water and sky; it re-collects in clouds to fall again to earth as the cycle continues. It is not a quick fix. It is a process that requires extended time.

The amount of water used every day is growing exponentially; more than ever in the history of humanity. Water is pulled from its sources faster than it has a chance to purify itself. Rivers are dredged and dammed, turned into straight channels, and used as liquid dumps for dangerous waste from human industry. Every year more and bigger disasters occur, further polluting the water. The names haunt us, specters of human horrors: the *Exxon Valdez* oil spill in Prince William Sound, the Deepwater Horizon oil rig explosion in the Gulf of Mexico, and Japan's Fukushima Daiichi nuclear power plant meltdown. Nuclear waste, oil, and toxic chemicals spew from broken tankers and underground pipes, fouling rivers, oceans, and all life within it. Rivers flooded with unnatural fuels burn as unnatural fire.

Massive forest fires, many caused by human negligence, burn through trees compromised by years of drought. High volumes of ash fall to the ground, clogging rivers, destroying water sheds, killing fish, and making water undrinkable.

As long ago as 1970 we started feeling the effects of acid rain—that horrible phenomenon caused by the water molecules in the atmosphere mixing with sulfur dioxide and nitrogen oxides released from too many factories belching noxious chemicals unchecked into the air. While this effect can occur naturally through lightning strikes or volcanic eruptions, acid rain from human pollution is far more prevalent and concentrated. The deadly rain falls to the earth, causing acidification of lakes and streams, killing all life within them. It also severely damages and even destroys trees in higher elevations.

The water needs our help. How are we doing? What are we doing? Are we ready to step up, able to take on the task?

Like the polluted waters of the planet, we have become overloaded with physical, psychic, mental, and emotional toxins. We need to take the time and find a way to process, cleanse, and purify our thoughts, emotions, and experiences. If we were to hold on to every event that ever occurred, their memories actively replaying in every moment, we would probably all be saturated with confusion and go crazy. We are told, and any therapist who assists in somatic work will verify, that our bodies hold memories in our cells that are primarily composed of water. Energy is never destroyed and perhaps neither are memories.

I wonder if there is a point at which water becomes so polluted that its memories are lost in the confusion. Is the increase in mental dementia happening because of water pollution? Perhaps our brains, floating in cerebrospinal fluid, have become flooded with toxic memories that have had no opportunity to be cleansed; like pollutants in a dredged out river, denied the purifying time in oxbow lakes.

We may be on memory overload but we do not have to carry every one of them with us or continue to attach fear, dread, or other negative emotions to them. Memories are, after all, the records of our experiences. Our experiences are what have shaped our lives. While we cannot change the experiences, we can change how we remember them.

We have the same basic transpiration system within us to purify and recycle our energy as the trees do. That system is our chakras. The universal light and love of Spirit flows into us like a cascading river, coursing down our spines, collecting in the energetic pools of our chakras, spreading out to refresh, revitalize, and rise through us again. We then send the life flow back out, recycling it, through our hearts, our actions, our words, our creativity, all we do. This cosmic recycling is a standard part of the law of attraction. We have to give it back so it can return. If we hold on to this energy, hoarding it, stashing it away deep within our bodies and minds, eventually our ability to receive the flow diminishes, like a river that has become clogged with flood debris. We become so much dead wood, weighed down by memories and experiences that no longer nourish us or lift us into higher consciousness.

Iridology studies the "tree rings" in our eyes. These distinct circles around the iris have been charted and shown to record disease, stress, and other conditions in our bodies. I wonder if we have chakra tree rings marking the years of struggle and poor growth in our lives, as well as periods of joy and personal transformation.

We are interconnected beings, sharing the same earth, air, water, space, and resources. Personal communication devices further link us, their electronic images flooding our brains. We all live in the same cosmic soup. The ash falling from a volcano in Iceland causes airlines to cancel flights, stranding passengers or forcing people on the other side of the planet to make sudden changes in plans. Nuclear waste in Japan shows up in cabbages in California. Along with the physical fallout of traumatic events, our resulting emotional reactions are spread like water. When we find ourselves experiencing deep grief or sadness for no apparent reason, it could be we are simply feeling the experiences of people left homeless in a disaster halfway across the world.

Are we being inundated with so much individual and global turmoil that a release of personal and collective memories is happening to us, just as with uprooted and broken trees immersed in flooded rivers? Are the roots of those memories being gently coaxed to the surface like an artesian spring, slowly bubbling up into the light, or are our memories being ripped out of us in chaos and stormy conditions?

As these memories flood our bodies, our awareness, our consciousness, they are revealed for a cosmic cleanup. I suggest we assist each other with love and compassion in this process. When the hidden is revealed, the reasons for the hiding are exposed. Opening to the flow of Spirit, allowing it to purify and transform us, moves us upward on the spiral of life to higher levels of light, love, awareness, and divine consciousness. Since our current thoughts, actions, and experiences become our future memories, we would be well served to keep a positive flow moving through us to create lives and resulting memories of joy, peace, and love. Perhaps somewhere deep within each of us, hidden under layers and lifetimes of human memory, our chakra tree rings are imprinted with the divine memories of God. And wouldn't they be wonderful to remember?

We are not like the trees who stand together in a forest. We move around, interacting with all of life: human, elemental, mineral, animal, and plant. We either access our light and love, freely giving it to others who then take it in and are nourished by it, or we deny the process, spreading our pollution. We live upon this beautiful Earth, Gaia. Although she and Spirit are able to provide unlimited resources for us, we must do our part to keep the flow moving. Cosmic recycling is about forgiveness. Charla told me forgiveness means *for giving away.* Just as we give away unwanted items to clear space in our homes, we give away that within us which is no longer useful, whether it be habits, memories, grudges, or fear, releasing the energy that has bound those conditions to us to be recycled into something better.

I like to think that my recycled insecurities are growing in a forest somewhere as beautiful, tall trees, calling in the rain.

26

Journey
Trees and Memories

⊚ Intention

Our intention for this journey is to travel inside a tree, access memories, and meet your tree guide.

Breathe out. Make some space. Breathe in, fill the space with your breath. Exhale. Release. Breathe in. Expand. Exhale. Free your breath. Breathe in. Expand and lighten yourself. Breathe out. Let your consciousness expand. Let your breath carry you.

You are walking in a beautiful forest. The ground is soft beneath your feet. It is quiet and peaceful here. The trees are very big and tall, reaching high up into the sky. Notice the trees and the sky. The air is cool. You can smell the rich scent of the trees. It feels good to be here—inviting, as if the trees are calling to you.

The lushness of the forest permeates your senses. You can smell and feel water in the air, in the damp ground. Perhaps water is

Tree roots in the Hoh Rain Forest, Washington

dripping from the trees. The forest floor is soft and spongy, with many layers of the leaves and needles of the trees, rotting bark from trees that fell long ago, mosses, and plants. Feel the softness, the beauty of the forest. Smell the richness of the forest, of the water, of the trees.

You experience a great sense of peace here; of a timeless belonging to this place, with these great trees, like a kinship with them. You feel at home here. You go up to trees to touch them, feeling their rough bark. Maybe you hug them, or simply rest your face against them, leaning into them, letting them support you. They feel so alive, so vibrant, so ancient.

There is a sound in the forest; a whispering, a sighing. Perhaps it is like soft singing or chanting. Listen. It is more than the wind moving through the trees. It is the trees communicating with each other, with the earth, with life. Listen to the trees. Can you hear them? Can you understand what they are saying?

As you listen to the trees you find one in particular that seems to draw you into its presence, into its energy field. This tree would like for you to come closer, to touch it, experience it. As you familiarize yourself with this tree you notice an opening at the base of the tree. Looking closer you see it is a doorway. As you watch, the door slowly opens, as if inviting you to enter. The door is open all the way now. Feeling safe and curious, you step through the door and find yourself inside the tree.

It is very big and open inside the tree. It is glowing with a blue, etheric light. The smell and sound of water is all around you; the smell of the tree. Your senses are flooded with these wonderful, earthy smells. There is a sense of wonder and awe at being inside this great tree.

You are standing on soft dirt. You shift your attention to your bare feet. Feel the earth under your feet, cool, moist. You see a dirt path leading downward. You step onto the path and begin to walk down deeper into the tree. The blue light makes it easy to see where you are going. What does it feel like to be walking inside this tree? Notice the sounds, the smells, the air around you.

As you continue downward on the path, you enter into the root system of the tree. At first the roots are small, reaching out in all directions. The deeper you go, the bigger the roots become until you reach the main and massive root system of the tree.

The path ends here, in the roots. Your feet wiggle in the rich, loamy dirt. It feels so wonderful to be here, you can feel the presence of Gaia in these roots, in the earth. Walk among the roots. Explore them. What do they feel like under your feet? Feel their texture, the thickness of them. You feel comfortable, safe here in the tree roots. A sense of timelessness settles into you. You have always been here. You will always be here. You dig your feet deeper among the roots, anchoring yourself within this great tree.

The roots are pulsing with water and nutrients. You can hear and feel the pull of the water moving through the tree, drawing from the roots, pulling the water and nutrients up through the tree. You can see the water moving through the tree. It flows vertically, like a river, a river inside the tree. You can hear it, smell it, and feel it. You realize it is the water in the tree that causes the etheric blue glow, the water that makes the tree shimmer with translucency.

This translucency allows you to see into the tree. There are layers in the sides of the tree, circular rings forming a column inside the tree. You are seeing the tree rings of this tree. They coalesce around this shimmering, watery energy. What do the tree rings look like?

As you become more attuned to the movement of the water, you can feel it moving through the roots and into your feet and up through your body. Feel the life of the tree moving through you. You look up. High above, you can see the leafy canopy of the tree reaching up to the sunlight far above you. From this perspective you can more clearly see the movement of the water flowing through the whole tree. The water forms a continuous spiral. It starts in the ground below you, slowly spiraling all the way through the tree. As you watch this flow, you realize you are looking at a watery staircase, slowly rising and spiraling upward. Yes, a moving stairway of water spiraling through the tree.

As you watch the stairs spiraling through the tree, you become aware of a being, a guide, standing on the stairs, moving toward you. A great feeling of love and wisdom emanates from the guide. Notice *all you can about her or him. Your tree guide has come to guide you to discover the memories of the tree, to discover your own memories. The watery stairs will carry you through the memories.*

Tree Guide invites you to step out onto those watery stairs. The guide reaches out a hand to assist you. What do the stairs feel like? With Tree Guide standing next to you, you are gently pulled up into the motion of the tree, into the energy of the tree. Experience the perfect order of this motion. As you slowly move on the stairs you pass through the tree's chakras—its tree rings. The energy in the tree rings circles through your body, aligning with your chakras. The water in the tree rings communicates with the water in your body. Your chakras begin to open to memories.

Aligned with the tree rings, you are drawn to stop, to listen, and to interact with the tree. The stairs will pause where you need them to, allowing you to access memories at different chakra centers. Perhaps you begin in the roots and find memories in your root chakra.

Feel the water and the tree's consciousness move through you. Open yourself to the memories that awaken in you. Let the tree and your tree guide support you. Let the water wash through you. Open yourself to the memories of who you are, of who you have been, and of who you are to become. Open yourself to the memories.

If you discover a memory you no longer wish to hold, simply let it flow into the water. The tree will take it and send it back, back to the earth where it will be recycled into a new form. Can you see your old memories being recycled?

Rise up through the chakra rings of the tree. Ride the watery stairs and find the next place you need to pause, to remember.

As the stairs move you through the tree, you share a consciousness with the water, with the tree. You understand that the tree is a sacred keeper of the memories—the memories of earth, sky, water, of all life that has passed this way. The tree would like to share its memories with you. Feeling the flow of the water through you, open up and allow the tree to share its memories with you. You can hear or feel the tree speaking to you. You can read the memory of the tree. What is the tree telling you? What is it showing you?

You are now invited to share your memories with the tree. The water carries the memories in the tree, carries the memories in you. The tree wants you to realize that you, too, are a sacred memory keeper. You hold memories within you that are critical not only to your life but to the life of all the beings of the earth. The tree invites you to access these memories in you now. What memories do you share with the tree?

The watery stairs have brought you to the heart of the tree now. The flow of water through the tree and through you blends together. You can feel the tree pulling the life force energy from below and above. The tree breathes in the great cosmic love of all that is, sends it through the water, and anchors it deep in its roots. Feel that love flowing through the water. Feel that love flow into you. Let the love purify you.

You continue to rise up the watery stairs, approaching the top of the tree where the leafy branches of the canopy spread out to capture the sunlight. You can feel the warmth of the sunlight. Finally, you reach the top, the crown of the tree. Looking out over the canopy of the tree you can see across the forest. What does it look like from this view at the top of the tree? What do you see? How do you feel? As the tree draws in the life force from the sun, you feel that same life force enter you through the top of your head, through your crown chakra, filling you with the brilliant divine light. Let yourself be filled with this light. Feel the full power of the tree moving through you. Feel your chakras open from the clearing of your memories. Feel your alignment with the tree, with Spirit.

The motion of the watery stairs is pulling you back down now. It is gently moving away from the top and starting your descent. Notice the inside of the tree as you move down. Can you see where limbs branch out? How the water flows to every part of the tree? You continue down the main shaft of the tree. The stairs will slow down and pause for you if you need them to. Enjoy the ride down.

You come back now to the roots of the tree. Stepping off the watery stairs you feel the earth beneath your feet. Looking up you see the stairs continuing their spiral journey up to the top of the tree and then coming back again, passing through the tree rings, moving the life force of the tree.

The water and the tree have a special gift for you. Tree Guide offers it to you now. What is the gift they have for you? Accept their gift and thank them. Ask them any questions you may have about it.

You find you have a gift to offer as well. What is it you offer to the water, to the tree guide, to the tree? Offer your gift now.

Take this time to ask any other questions you may have of the tree, the water, or your tree guide. Tree Guide assures you that you may return here anytime you would like to. The tree, the water, and Tree Guide will always remember you, will always be available to help you process your memories; but for now, it is time to go.

Expressing your love and gratitude, you turn back through the roots to the dirt path, following it up and out of the tree roots. Ahead of you is the door you came through. It opens and you walk through it and are back in the forest. As you begin to walk away you hear the trees talking. You know you will always be a part of them, a part of this forest; sharing your memories with the trees, the water, the earth.

And you find yourself back in this time and space. Breathing in. Breathing out. Breathing your watery breath and holding the water and the trees in your heart.

Deepening Your Practice

This journey is presented with the primary intention of experiencing the water and chakra rings of the tree you visit to help you access memories. However, trees are wise and loving beings with many gifts to offer us. A variation you might want to try is to ask your tree guide to take you to a specific tree for a particular need you might have at this time. Maybe you want to go back to an old favorite tree from childhood to help you remember events from that time, simply for the pleasure of recalling happy days as a child. Or, you could journey with the intention to remember blocked memories around a childhood trauma that you feel needs to be accessed and released. If you chose this kind of journey, please have someone with you to offer you support.

Or, if you have an illness, or are exploring ways to support others who have an illness, you might shift the intention to ask to be taken to a tree that might offer its unique healing qualities to help with that condition. For example, a eucalyptus might help with sinus congestion. A yew tree might offer assistance for cancer, a cedar or melaleuca tree could offer purification. Prior research into the healing properties of trees would be beneficial not only in this journey but for a prolonged health regime. If you do not know which tree might best help a condition you have, you may simply invoke your tree guide to lead you to the tree best for you at this time.

27

Forest Fires in Montana

IN THE SUMMER OF 2000 the Bitterroot Mountains around Missoula, Montana, were on fire. The TV news reports showed footage of a flaming mountainside choking with clouds of thick smoke. A crisply dressed news reporter gazed knowingly into the camera, speaking scripted words of assurance to the public. "Forest fires are a natural process that assist in forest renewal," he droned, "if they stay small and contained. Diseased trees burn away, allowing new growth." Turning to face a different camera angle, he adjusted his glasses with a professorial nudge to the nosepiece. "Grasses sprout up from the burned-off debris of dead brush, fallen tree limbs, and layers of dried pine needles." Looking like he was sharing a great secret, he continued, "Some seeds cannot be released from pine cones without the intense heat of a forest fire."

All well and good in Forestry 101; however, the Bitterroot fire was ravaging through acres of forest that was suffering from a long drought and had not had a major burn in years. Bone dry, it was burning hot and fast. The lives and homes of people and animals were threatened and being destroyed. Thinking about the fires was distressing. Being a tree lover my whole life, I could not bear to think about the once verdant forest reduced to smoldering, black-ened trunks.

I called my friend Sylvia to enlist her help. She and I had been getting together fairly regularly to practice shamanic journeywork; seeking the assistance of spirit guides to transport us to other realms of consciousness for visionary support in healing, mostly in personal transformation but also for the planet. She agreed to come over to my house. It was a Friday night and neither of us had to work the next day.

Waiting for her arrival I asked Spirit what I could do to help. I offered myself to be in service for the Standing People, the trees.

The doorbell rang. Sylvia had arrived. I welcomed her with a quick hug. She dumped her coat and purse on the couch and we headed down the hall to the altar room. The welcoming peace of a place dedicated to prayer and ceremony reached out to us. We lit candles and sat down on the floor, talking about the fires. It was just so hot and dry in Montana. If only it would rain! We agreed to journey together, shamanically, to the fire area to see if we could bring rain. Well, why not? It seemed like a reasonable idea even though I had never engaged in any kind of rain dance, cloud busting, or other weather-related ritu-als. Feeling a sense of wonder and excitement, we smudged each other, clearing off the energies of our busy day, and brought our focus to ceremony.

We faced each direction, invoking the guardians and spirits of each spiritual doorway, creating a sacred circle. Next we announced our intention to be of assistance to stop the fires in Montana and to bring rain, if it was for the highest good of the area.

I removed the silver tray covering the sacred water altar so that the water and crystal inside the glass bowl were exposed to our words and energies. I began to stir the waters with the selenite wand. With Sylvia's focus and energy aligned with mine, I slipped out into another realm of consciousness, moving up and out into the atmosphere. I could feel the cool air of Seattle around me but focused my attention eastward, navigating through time and space.

The altar room fell away; Seattle was in some far, distant place. The air was getting warmer and thicker. I saw the glow of fires below me and called out to the elemental spirits: "Great beings of the west! Thunder beings! Guardians of the rain! I call on you and thank you for your gifts to us of the rains! We need you now! The trees, the

The author's west altar at night

great Standing People, are on fire. The animals are panicked and have lost their homes. They run madly away from these burning flames. Many have died. The homes of the humans are burning. The clear water of the river reflects the flames jumping from tree to tree. We need your help!"

Going deeper into my vision I saw myself in the midst of a changing weather pattern above the fires. Raising my arms, I invoked the water vapors, calling on them to coalesce into clouds. Massive clouds formed and roiled around me. "Yes! Thank you, Cloud People. Fill with water! Mighty winds! Carry the clouds over the fires and position them to cover the blazes below them. Please, great Mother God, for the highest good, let the rains come. We need the rain to quench the fires."

The vision shifted. Sylvia was now next to me in this Spirit realm. Two great eagles flying through the skies carried us on their backs, their strong wings moving us upward, forward, and into the storm clouds that were forming around us. We carried drums and rattles, beating and shaking them in synchronized rhythm to the booming thunder, our faces illuminated by flashes of lightning. We called out an ancient invocation but the sound of our voices was lost in the noise of the tempest. The storm grew in intensity. The electrically charged air created static causing the hair on our heads to fly out around us. Wild, eerie electricity crackled around us as our eagles continued to circle the blackening clouds, carrying us on this shamanic storm flight.

The heat from the fires below was rising up. Flames lit up the bottoms of the clouds as lightning outlined the edges.

"Come on rain! You great mystery of the gods! Bring your mighty gift of water to these trees, to these animals, to these people! We call on you to end the burning!"

Wind and water continued to rush together like lost souls reuniting. Ozone, ions, hydrogen, oxygen whirling in ancient alchemy. The clouds filled with water, hoarding their precious cargo until the winds moved them just so.

And the rain fell. Like pockets cut with a knife of pure light, the water escaped its cloudy bonds dropping toward Earth. The intense heat of the fires created a barrier, blocking the moisture from reaching the ground. A great sizzling occurred. Mountains of steam billowed up and were sucked back by the thunder beings into even larger clouds to condense again into water. Again the rain fell. Faster now, and with more eagerness to reach land as if its initial attempt merely whet its own appetite.

This time the volume of the rain held together. The higher levels of heat from the fires sucked up the water, barely giving way. More and more of the precious liquid hurled itself out of celestial cisterns. The rain began to pass through the fire, flame by flame, hissing and sputtering in the unrelenting downpour. Great volumes of steam engulfed us on our never faltering eagles, their screeching cries audible over the noise of the storm. Sylvia and I were also howling, adding our spirit voices to the fray.

Splat. Splop. Raindrops began to reach the ground. One, two, then a torrent of water carried in individual droplets, each a miracle, a gift no human could ever imitate. Flaming tongues of fire hissed and transformed into steamy vapor. The hot and parched ground gasped and opened itself to receive the long-awaited drink. Trees cheered, knowing they would not have to hold out against the carnage much longer. Animals turned in flight, sensing relief.

The rain gathered itself into a steady but gentle downpour. Thunder rolled and growled like angry bears. The lightning, as if realizing the forest had already had enough fire, stayed well above, playing at some kind of atmospheric red rover game, flashing light from cloud to cloud. The rain settled in like a mother having a long cry over the pain of her children. It will be all right. It will be all right.

The unrelenting gale finally calmed to a breeze. Smoke and darkness cleared away. Soft hues of pink and purple filled my vision. The great eagles gently deposited us into a cloud of color and turned to fly away into the west. We were rocked back and forth in the currents of clear, fresh air. Up and down. In and out. Inhale. Exhale. Breathing. My breath.

We were back.

"Oh my word, Raven. Did you see that? Did you see it?" Sylvia cried.

My hand was still holding the selenite wand, my arm still stirring the water in the water altar bowl. I stopped and let go of the wand, letting it slide back into the water. Turning to look at Sylvia helped me shift back from vision mode to the physical world again.

"Yes. I saw it. We were flying on eagles. The rain came. The fires went out."

We looked at each other in amazement. As if reading each other's thoughts, we both held up our arms and offered our deep gratitude to the guides for this amazing journey. Closing our circle, we extinguished the candles and left the altar room.

I made a pot of tea. We sat in the dining room, silently sipping the herbal brew. Then, I spoke. "Sylvia. I have to go to Montana. Right away."

"What? Why?"

"I have to go there with the water altar. I want to give massages to the firefighters. I have a friend in Missoula. I will call her in the morning."

True to my vow, I called my friend, Penny, and asked her if she would help. We had gone to massage school together back in 1989. A few years following our graduation, she had moved to Missoula where she now had a successful massage practice. She told me she had been wanting to go to the fire camps, too. I should just come and we would figure out the details when I got there.

I went into my clinic Monday morning, taking only the first two of my appointments, canceling all the rest for the entire week.

I was on a mission.

I packed up the car, including all the elixir from the water altar, and hit the road. On the way out I bought a Krishna Das CD and spent the entire trip chanting to the music, staying in focus. I stopped only as necessary, keeping the vision in my mind, following my purpose.

Heading east on I-40, the miles through Washington and Idaho went by quickly. As I entered Montana, I noticed the forest access roads off the freeway were all closed. Signs stating Fire Danger High reminded the traveler of the precarious world outside the comfort of an air-conditioned vehicle. I wondered about any local eagles. Were their arboreal homes burned? Had they all flown to safe refuge?

I finally arrived in Missoula. The whole town was filled with a smoky haze. The acrid smell made my nose feel stuffy, irritated the back of my throat, stung my eyes. Citizens were being advised to stay indoors except for necessary excursions.

Penny and I were delighted to see each other again. Ignoring the smoke advisory, we had dinner at a local restaurant, happily catching up on each other's activities. The next morning we loaded up her truck with whatever we thought we might need as volunteer massage therapists and went in search of the fire camps. We both had our tables, oils, lotions, bolsters, blankets. Her truck was soon filled with the tools of our trade along with extra clothing, food, and water.

And, of course, the bottles filled from the water altar.

Full of a sense of adventure, with no agenda other than finding a fire camp, we headed out of town and drove up into the Bitterroot Mountains toward the fires. Somehow Penny navigated us to our destination. After driving about an hour we found one of the camps, a large government-run facility where military personnel and local residents hired as temporary workers provided the services needed to support troops of firefighters. Of course, there was a guard at the front of the camp. We announced we were massage therapists and had come to offer our services. Would they like the two best therapists in Washington and Montana to join them?

The young man dressed in camos looked at us skeptically. "Sure, ladies. Wait here."

He went off to find someone in charge. We just tagged along. Neither of us was very good at waiting around. A man in uniform, walking with the purposeful stride of someone in charge, came to talk to us and checked out the truck. We told our story again. I tactfully did not mention my intention to perform ceremony with the water altar elixir. We assured him we were here as volunteers and expected no money. We could see our arrival was puzzling to him. You could almost hear his rational mind checking off all the possibilities. Why would these two women show up here? What are they up to? If we take them on, is the government responsible for them?

We definitely were not in the protocol manuals.

Perhaps it was Spirit guiding his thoughts; perhaps his aching muscles, sensing well-trained hands working out the knots in his neck and shoulders, overrode his need to adhere to government regulations. Whatever the process, he decided we were for real and set about finding a place for us to stay. A spare tent, a couple of GI sleeping bags, a makeshift sign that read FREE MASSAGE, and we were in business!

The camp was like a small town complete in itself. A large tent for a cafeteria had rows of long tables covered with plastic tablecloths, folding chairs neatly arranged along the sides, waiting for hungry people to pull up a seat and enjoy a meal planned to provide just the right amount of calories per government regulations. A "reefer-rig," which was more like a giant freezer pulled by a semi-truck, held huge amounts of frozen foods; a bank of refrigerators hooked to generators hummed in the Montana heat. A full staff of cooks provided meals to all the firefighters and workers, with others performing duties of dishwashing and general cleanup. A snack station was kept stocked all day so anyone could have a cold drink or granola bar if they got hungry.

Other tents were set up in neat rows, serving as offices for all the paperwork generated by this operation. Portable showers and a laundry area kept people clean. The well-equipped medical tent was ready to serve the many injuries expected from the strenuous and dangerous hours out on the fire line. A large communication tent where the fire locations were pinpointed on a huge topographical map also housed a giant-screen TV where people could watch movies in the evening. There was even a Black Hawk helicopter perched nearby, its handsome pilot creating a flurry of flirting from the female enlisted who were fawning for rides.

During the day the firefighters were farther up the mountain battling the blazes. Rows of tents for individual sleepers, filled with cots or sleeping bags, were neatly made up and ready for their return after a day of hard physical and emotional labor.

Our appearance in the camp created quite a stir. Everyone was thrilled to have us. We set up shop near the medical tent and started giving massages to those running the camp. By the time the exhausted, and sometimes injured, men and women returned from the fires at night, they were ready to eat and go to sleep. Finding the newest addition to their camp was a great surprise for them. Penny and I spent long hours into the night standing over our tables massaging sore muscles, helping to ease pain and stress. Each person we helped was truly grateful. It was an incredible and rewarding experience.

The lines got longer every night and we turned no one away. One man had been waiting for several hours. He kept intently watching me with eyes that seemed to look right into me; like he knew me. I kept returning his gaze, feeling a connection with him on a deep level. It was not a romantic feeling; more like a recognition of souls. When it was finally his turn, he would be my last massage of the night. Before saying anything to me, he held out his hand. In it was a small bundle of fresh tobacco leaves wrapped in a piece of red cloth. Recognizing this as an offering one would make to an elder or spiritual leader, I asked him his name.

"Jeb, from Oklahoma—Cherokee country."

I thanked him and accepted his gift, making an offering gesture to Spirit by raising the bundle upwards in my hands.

"I am honored, Jeb, that you bring this to me," I said, looking into eyes that seemed very wise for his young years. "I am a ceremonialist and will use this tobacco as an offering."

Never taking his eyes off mine, he nodded and said, "I see who you are." And I felt seen; acknowledged. Here was one person who somehow knew I came here to do more than massages.

With that exchange, he got on the table, had his treatment, and went out into the night. I thought of the vision that had brought me here to do this work and how everything had fallen into place so easily to allow me to be here. I could feel Spirit at work around me, and through me. Sometimes we get to see ourselves through someone else's eyes. I had that moment with Jeb. It felt good. I never saw him again but I shall not forget his gift to me.

After three days at camp, Penny returned to her clients in town. I rode in with her and drove my car back up to the camp where I continued to work alone for the next two days. Now it was time for me to go, too. The entire time I had been in Montana, the days were scorching hot, the nights barely cooling down. Smoke was a constant presence.

It was time to go to the river.

I packed up the car, said goodbye to my new friends, and headed down the mountain.

Nearby was a perfect access to the Bitterroot River. I parked the car, shouldered the daypack that held the bottles filled with the water altar elixir, and walked down the convenient path to the river. The water was beautiful, clear, cold, and gleaming in the sunlight. It was such a welcome relief from the parched air and ground of the fire camp. Large pine trees grew here, offering their green beauty and gift of shade. Finding a low area of the river, I waded out onto a sand spit where I could sit and watch the water flow around me. Removing my boots and socks, I settled my hot and tired feet into the cold water. I offered my thanks and blessings to the water. It was good to sit here and listen to the bubbling cadence of the river as it flowed over the rocks; watching the water part and divide and rejoin itself again. I recalled the journey Sylvia and I had taken in my altar room just over a week ago, reliving the wild ride on the back of the great eagle into the storm and how the rains had fallen, quenching the fires.

Opening each bottle of the sacred water elixir, I slowly poured the contents into the river; praying for the end of the fires, for the rain to come, for the renewal of the forest, for the waters to be healed and restored. I visualized water, tinted orange and red from reflecting burning trees, become streaked with amethyst-colored sparkles from the elixir.

I felt a great peace within me, a feeling of surrender. I heard the call. I had the vision. I came here and did my work. Reluctant to leave, but knowing I had hours of driving ahead of me, I let my feet dry in the sun, put my socks and boots back on, crossed the river, and went back to the car. Time to go home.

Shortly after crossing the Washington border, I decided to take a detour out into the vast wheat fields that covered the area like a thick golden blanket. Driving down an empty farm road that led into the heart of the fields, I parked and got out of the car. It was totally quiet here except for the sound of the wind and an occasional bird. Leaning against the car, I closed my eyes, soaking up the sun. The peaceful silence was suddenly broken by a loud and familiar sound. I looked up. Two golden eagles were flying above my head, performing aerial acrobatics. Diving, swooping, rising, soaring, calling, they danced together across the huge blue sky. Their grace, power, and beauty was beyond description. I was completely captivated by them. What a gift to be their witness.

The ground seemed to shift under my feet. For a moment, I felt I was up there with them; perched atop a strong feathered back, propelled by powerful wings, riding out the storm.

After perhaps ten or fifteen minutes of their lofty display, the eagles realigned themselves with the thermals and started to spiral up and away from me until I finally lost sight of them.

I got back into my car, returned to the main highway, and continued my drive home. I was tired but felt contented, happy. Somewhere near Seattle my cell phone rang. It was Penny, telling me that it was raining over the Bitterroots.

Closing Thoughts

IT IS MY HOPE that this book has inspired each of you to become more intentional about your relationship with water. There is not a second of our lives that is not dependent on water. From the water in our bodies, to the water we drink, cook with, bathe in, cool our homes with, or use in unlimited ways, water is critical to us and to every being on the planet. No one can live without it. Look around you the next time you go anywhere—down the freeway, around your neighborhood, at work, school, in nature. Every single thing you see is dependent on water. It is either kept alive by water or was man-made using water in the process. Nothing exists without water. It is part of everything. Even fire contains some water vapor.

I remember, as a kid in Wyoming, going hiking with my family in the mountains. If we were thirsty, we just knelt down at the edge of a mountain stream, put our faces in the crystal clean water and drank our fill. By the time I was in my twenties you couldn't do that anymore because of Giardia parasites in the water. People started getting really sick and were shocked to discover we could not drink our mountain water anymore.

The problem has only worsened every year. Contributing factors include oil spills in pristine waters; napalm in the redwood forests;

flooding from extreme weather conditions; droughts; and fires followed by rains that wash the fire retardants down land stripped of vegetation, eroding the soil, rushing into fields and dumping dirt and toxins into the water tables. In addition there is rampant construction and development that tears up natural lands, cuts down trees, and damages watersheds. Tract housing is built on flood plains, woodlands are turned into gated communities, and residents are shocked when water, its natural channels lost, drains through their yards or living rooms.

More people are using water for both private and industrial needs. And now we have hydrofracking, a dangerous way of extracting natural gas from deep wells in the expansive shale beds of the earth. Drilling down as much as 8,000 feet (the drinking aquifers are at about 1,000 feet), millions of gallons of water mixed with sand and a deadly cocktail of an estimated 596 chemicals are inserted under very high pressure into the natural gas wells to fracture the shale and release gas deposits not accessible by conventional drilling. The dirty residue and gas leaks into the aquifers causing contamination to drinking water, making it gritty and reeking with foul, methane smells. Some people have found they can literally light their drinking water on fire as it pours out of the faucets in their homes. Due to political favoritism, hydrofracking is exempt from the 1974 Safe Drinking Water Act and so frackers do not have to reveal what those chemicals are. However, scientists have identified enough of them to know the fracking cocktail is definitely bad news. Benzene, xylene, toluene, and ethylbenzene have all been found in the mix. Some of these are naturally occurring organic chemicals but the problem is when they are combined with other chemicals (and we don't know exactly what is being used in hydrofracking). The chemical combo targets and adversely affects the central nervous system causing a wide array of problems. Liver and kidney failure, birth defects, spontaneous abortions, and carcinogens related to leukemia, are all related to these chemicals.

Each fracking event takes 1–8 million gallons of water. A well can be fracked up to eighteen times. That could mean 144 million gallons of water being contaminated on just one well. Evaporating equipment runs twenty-four hours a day every day to try to rid the water of the highly volatile organic chemicals. Finally, the water is taken to wastewater treatment plants to be recycled back into the public supply and released into our waterways. How clean do you think it really gets?

It is a toxic world out there. It can be overwhelming to think about it. With its natural purification cycle lost to all our human interference, how can water re-collect its wholeness? Its purity?

We humans can be the vessel for Spirit as well as the agent of destruction. You can make a difference. Every time you go out with your sacred water elixir offering your prayers for the water you help transform the damage. Every prayer you offer, every effort you make helps to not only offset this destruction but to turn it around. You become the altar. You become the vessel. You become the pure flow of Spirit on the earth.

My good Mormon parents followed the church rule of having a two-year supply of food on hand. Our basement was loaded with floor-to-ceiling shelves crammed with large, sealed cans of dehydrated food amongst the other extensive stash of canned goods, two freezers full of foil-wrapped mysteries, and tons (yes, tons) of wheat and corn. As a joke, my dad purchased a case of empty cans labeled, "Dehydrated Water. Open can. Add water." We thought it was hilarious. But the truth is, we cannot make water. We cannot make any of the basics of life. We can grow corn from seeds but we cannot make the seed. The resources of life, of the Earth, are freely given to us by our Creator. We have free will and may use them as we choose. It is up to us to give back to life by remembering to honor and bless these gifts as we use them. As in any relationship, if all we do is take and never reciprocate, we will use up the good will of that relationship. The Earth seems ultimately patient with us but do we really want to find out if there is a point of no return?

The sacred water altar is a complete alchemy lab. All four of the basic elements are involved. The earth is represented in the vessel, the crystals, and the physical altar. The air is your breath, your words, your prayers. The fire comes from your love, your will, your decision to take action. The water is present in the water poured over those crystals as well as the water inside the crystals themselves, and the water inside you, in your breath. A great alchemy occurs in bringing the elements together, stirring in your intention, and offering the elixir of transformation back to Gaia. The natural, creative flow of life is a movement from order to chaos and back to order. It is always changing but always seeking homeostasis, balance. We humans are constantly participating in that process. Our intentional awareness is what can make us alchemists of positive change, consciously contributing to harmony, balance, beauty.

You don't have to be overwhelmed, and you don't have to be perfect. The sacred water is a simple way to help the water, to help Gaia. As the waters of the planet heal and move into us, we become healthier. The more positive the flow of water is, the more positive the flow of energy will be. The sacred water altar helps increase our awareness of how we use our precious water and how we treat our relationship with it. Every moment is a new beginning. Turn your intention, your love, and your energy back to the water.

Thank you, Water, for your gift of life. I see you clean and restored.

Notes

CHAPTER 11. WORKING THE ALTAR

1. Melody, *Love Is in the Earth* (Wheat Ridge, Colo.: Earth Love Publishing House, 1995), 109–12.
2. Ibid., 594–95.

CHAPTER 15. OUR WATER ON DRUGS

1. "Even the Sound Is Getting a Caffeine Buzz," *Seattle Times,* 3 July 2000.
2. Ibid.
3. Gary G. Kohls, "Pharma Invades Water Supplies," April 20, 2010, www .consortiumnews.com/2010/042010b.html.
4. Ibid.
5. Ibid.

CHAPTER 19. DR. EMOTO

1. Masaru Emoto, *Messages from Water* (Tokyo, Japan: HADO Kyoikusha, 1999).
2. Ibid., 130.
3. Ibid.

Recommended Reading

I cannot possibly know or mention all the great reading opportunities out there. As the saying goes—so many books, so little time. Here are a few books I recommend.

Ellis, Normandi. *Awakening Osiris: The Egyptian Book of the Dead*. San Francisco: Red Wheel/Weiser, 2009.

———. *Feasts of Light: Celebrations for the Seasons of Life*. Wheaton, Ill.: Quest Books, 1999.

———. *Imagining the World into Existence: An Ancient Egyptian Manual of Consciousness*. Rochester, Vt.: Bear & Company, 2012.

Ellis, Normandi, and Gloria Taylor Brown. *Invoking the Scribes of Ancient Egypt: The Initiatory Path of Spiritual Journeying*. Rochester, Vt.: Bear & Company, 2011.

Judith, Anodea. *Wheels of Life: A User's Guide to the Chakra System*. St. Paul, Minn.: Llewellyn, 1992.

Neihardt, John G. *Black Elk Speaks: Being the Life Story of a Holy Man of the Oglala Sioux*. As told through John G. Neihardt. Lincoln: University of Nebraska Press, 1932.

Outwater, Alice. *Water: A Natural History.* New York: Basic Books, 1996.

Scully, Nicki. *Alchemical Healing: A Guide to Spiritual, Physical, and Transformational Medicine.* Rochester, Vt.: Bear & Company, 2003.

Scully, Nicki, and Mark Hallert. *Planetary Healing: Spirit Medicine for Global Transformation.* Rochester, Vt.: Bear & Company, 2011.

Index

Page numbers in *italics* refer to illustrations.

BOOKS OF RELATED INTEREST

Planetary Healing
Spirit Medicine for Global Transformation
by Nicki Scully and Mark Hallert

The Spiritual Life of Water
Its Power and Purpose
by Alick Bartholomew

Original Instructions
Indigenous Teachings for a Sustainable Future
Edited by Melissa K. Nelson

Plant Spirit Healing
A Guide to Working with Plant Consciousness
by Pam Montgomery

Wisdom of the Plant Devas
Herbal Medicine for a New Earth
by Thea Summer Deer

Thomas Berry, Dreamer of the Earth
The Spiritual Ecology of the Father of Environmentalism
Edited by Ervin Laszlo and Allan Combs

The Healing Power of Energized Water
The New Science of Potentizing the World's Most Vital Resource
by Ulrich Holst

Moonrise
The Power of Women Leading from the Heart
Edited by Nina Simons with Anneke Campbell

Inner Traditions • Bear & Company
P.O. Box 388
Rochester, VT 05767
1-800-246-8648
www.InnerTraditions.com

Or contact your local bookseller